LEAD!

Becoming an Effective Coach and Mentor to Your Nursing Staff

Patty Kubus, RN, MBA, PhD

Lead! Becoming an Effective Coach and Mentor to Your Nursing Staff is published by HCPro, Inc.

Copyright © 2010 HCPro, Inc.

Cover Images: © StockLite, 2010 Used under license from Shutterstock.com; © iStockphoto.com/Dale Hogan; © Photos.com/Getty Images

ISBN: 978-1-60146-780-5

HCPro, Inc., provides information resources for the healthcare industry.

HCPro, Inc., is not affiliated in any way with The Joint Commission, which owns the JCAHO and Joint Commission trademarks. MAGNET™, MAGNET RECOGNITION PROGRAM®, and ANCC MAGNET RECOGNITION® are trademarks of the American Nurses Credentialing Center (ANCC). The products and services of HCPro, Inc., and The Greeley Company are neither sponsored nor endorsed by the ANCC. The acronym MRP is not a trademark of HCPro or its parent corporation.

Patty Kubus, RN, MBA, PhD, Author
Rebecca Hendren, Senior Managing Editor
Mike Briddon, Executive Editor
Emily Sheahan, Group Publisher
Janell Lukac, Graphic Artist

Sada Preisch, Proofreader
Susan Darbyshire, Art Director
Matt Sharpe, Production Supervisor
Jean St. Pierre, Senior Director of Operations

Advice given is general. Readers should consult professional counsel for specific legal, ethical, or clinical questions. Arrangements can be made for quantity discounts. For more information, contact:

HCPro, Inc.
75 Sylvan Street, Suite A-101
Danvers, MA 01923
Telephone: 800/650-6787 or 781/639-1872
Fax: 800/639-8511
E-mail: *customerservice@hcpro.com*

Visit HCPro online at:
www.hcpro.com and *www.hcmarketplace.com*

CONTENTS

Lead! Becoming an Effective Coach and Mentor to Your Nursing Staff   **iii**

© 2010 HCPro, Inc.

Contents

Lead! Becoming an Effective Coach and Mentor to Your Nursing Staff

© 2010 HCPro, Inc.

v

ABOUT THE AUTHOR

Patty Kubus, RN, MBA, PhD

As President of Leadership Potential International, Inc., Patty Kubus, RN, MBA, PhD, focuses her skills and experience on executive coaching, leadership development, career planning, team building, and cultural change initiatives. She has more than 25 years of experience leading others and consulting, and her clients include many Fortune 500 corporate executives, from directors to C-level leaders. Her experience crosses many industries, including healthcare, academia, hospitality, finance, technology, and pharmaceuticals.

In addition to her consulting experience, she has management experience as a nurse manager, a role in which she managed a large team of critical care nurses at a university medical center, and as a district sales manager for a global pharmaceutical company, a role in which she managed a team of sales consultants. As an assistant professor of management, she managed the human resource management curriculum at a private college in Pennsylvania, where she taught HR and leadership courses.

Her educational background includes a Bachelor of Science in Nursing from St. Mary's College of Notre Dame, an MBA from Boston College, and a Doctorate in Human Development and Education from Marywood University.

Her recent speaking engagements include the Sigma Theta Tau Nursing Leadership Summit in Atlanta and the Georgia Hospital Pharmacy Association annual meeting, where she presented "Leadership Lessons from the Dance Floor." She has been a guest on the PBS radio show *At Work* where she was interviewed on the topic of organizational culture.

She gives back to her community by being a frequently sought-after speaker at numerous job seeker/professional development events, where she presents workshops on "Creating and Networking Your Brand" and "Planning for a Behavioral Interview."

She can be reached at *www.leadershippotentialintl.com.*

ACKNOWLEDGMENTS

I want to express my heartfelt appreciation to all those who helped me while writing this book. I am deeply grateful to my friends and colleagues who shared their ideas with me, reviewed the manuscript, and provided support during this endeavor including Barb Cox-Geyer, Diane Mass, Barry Hawthorne, Marc Todd, Maura Stewart, Dr. Dirk Baxter, Dr. Andy Neiner, Marianne Craft, Mike Andrew, Viviana Brantley, Cynthia Smith, and Karen Stanley, who put me in contact with my wonderful editor, Rebecca Hendren.

This book is dedicated to my mother, Esther Hogan Kubus, who dressed me up as a nurse for my first Halloween when I was two-years-old.

All the tools and templates in the book are online so you can adapt and use them at your facility. The files are available as Word documents so they may be easily customized and are organized by figure number in the book.

Find the tools online at:

www.hcpro.com/downloads/8984

Continuing Education Credits Available

Continuing education credits are available for this book for two years from date of purchase.

For more information about credits available, and to take the continuing education exam, please see the Nursing Education Instructional Guide found at the end of the book.

CHAPTER 1

THE PATH TO BECOMING AN AUTHENTIC LEADER

Learning Objectives

After reading this chapter, the reader will be able to:

- Define authentic leadership
- List the five dimensions of authentic leadership
- Explain why self-awareness is a necessary competency for authentic leaders

Nursing leaders, including nurse managers, charge nurses, service directors, nurse executives, educators, and chief nursing officers, are facing pressures like never before. These pressures include quality improvement, retention of staff, research, staff development, financial constraints, safety, communication with team members, short- and long-term planning, new technology, competition, increased patient acuity, and changes to the healthcare delivery system.

With so many demands on nurse leaders, it is understandable that you might find yourself reacting to the most pressing crisis of the day, rather than taking the time to occasionally pull back and reflect on ways to maximize your skills and proactively help your team navigate this complex environment.

This chapter discusses taking the time to look in the mirror and define your authentic leadership style for the enrichment of yourself and all of those around you.

Understanding Authentic Leadership

In today's world, where we see too many self-serving leaders who try to work the system to get their agendas pressed forward for their own fortune and fame, you can become discouraged in your attempt to achieve your goals to make a positive difference in the world.

Time and time again, we see leaders making decisions from a position of greed: from financial meltdowns on Wall Street to the multimillion-dollar golden parachutes and bonuses given to executives who have decimated the lives of their employees, vendors, and communities. What we read in the news is not the way most of us want to live our lives and be remembered.

The need for authentic leaders is greater than ever and we cannot be thwarted by what makes the news.

Authentic leadership is important for several reasons. Authentic leaders are not driven toward self-serving interests. They are motivated by a goal that is not about them but is about the greater good. They have the self-knowledge to understand their gifts (talents) and passions and are committed to empowering others to use their gifts and passions to accomplish a shared goal that will benefit others.

Authentic leaders become powerful by giving power to others and allowing others to use their skills and talents to their fullest potential. As we learned from Abraham Maslow, our loftiest need is self-actualization. Authentic leaders aspire to become self-actualized, and they are committed to helping others satisfy this need in themselves. That's powerful for everyone.

The path to authentic leadership is circuitous, bumpy, and constant. There is no end point to the journey. It is a continuous learning process of discovery, trial, and error. One of the first requirements is a commitment to developing self-awareness. In fact, many leaders believe that self-awareness is the most important ability for leadership (George, 2007). Without clear self-awareness, you can take the wrong path and end up chasing the "glitter," thus not holding true to your values. It also makes it difficult to relate well to others and empathize with them when you don't have a clear understanding of your strengths, weaknesses, and pressure points (George, 2007).

Becoming an authentic leader begins with taking a rigorous inventory of your strengths, limitations, motivations, values, knowledge, and experience. Think about yours right now. It is surprising how many people cannot come up with a list or think of even a few of their own strengths and limitations. How can you accept yourself and develop a plan to grow so you can meet increasing challenges if you don't even know who you are? How can you follow a path and lead others if you don't know which path to take?

The problem is that while many people, for a variety of reasons, can become leaders, many tend to bounce from obstacle to obstacle for years, wondering why their heads hurt and what to do about the damage they leave in their wakes. By becoming self-aware, an authentic leader will ensure avoidance of these mistakes. Authentic leaders still encounter obstacles, but they see these situations as feedback that allows them to learn, grow, and help others grow.

Self-Awareness

"You are unique, and if that is not fulfilled, then something has been lost."
—*Martha Graham*

It is important to have self-awareness before you can be "other-aware" (Covey, 1994). You can't listen to and support someone else's heart and dreams if you are blind to your own. This is the foundation of authentic leadership.

Start by reflecting on the following:

- Your values

- Your motivations (needs and fears)

- Your strengths

- Your limitations (we all have them)

Values

Identifying and living by our values helps us in many ways. One benefit is that know-ing your values makes decision-making easier. When you have clear values, you can filter any decision through them as a first pass. For example, if one of your personal values is health, your values will filter the options on a restaurant menu, which will narrow your choices and save you time.

Living your values helps you build trusting relationships with others because your behavior will be consistent. Most of us like consistency when working with others.

Authentic leaders always value honesty. Let's say you start a new job, and contrary to what the hiring supervisor said in the interview, he actually turns out to be a micro-manager. Trust is breached, since what he said is not congruent with how he acts. How likely are you to be open and honest with this person when you can't trust him? Communication will quickly shut down unless you decide to confront him.

Values identification exercise

If you are not clear on your personal values, take the time to devote an uninterrupted period to focus on a values identification exercise. Get a list of values (you can find a variety online) and go through the list one value at a time. See Figure 1.1 for a sample list you can use. The list of values is not exhaustive. You can find the tool in the down-loadable resources section, which contains all the tools in this book (find it at *www.hcpro.com/downloads/8984*). Download and add any values you want.

FIGURE 1.1 ■ PERSONAL VALUES EXERCISE							
Value	**Yes or No**	**Value**	**Yes or No**	**Value**	**Yes or No**	**Value**	**Yes or No**
Accomplishment		Accountability		Accuracy		Achievement	
Ambition		Autonomy		Challenge		Collaboration	
Compassion		Competency		Courage		Credibility	
Creativity		Dedication		Dependability		Dignity	
Discipline/order		Diversity		Enjoyment/fun		Efficiency	
Empathy		Equality		Excellence		Excitement	
Family		Freedom		Friendliness		Flexibility	
Generosity		Health		Honesty		Improvement	
Independence		Individuality		Influence		Innovativeness	
Integrity		Learning		Loyalty		Optimism	
Persistence		Quality		Respect		Responsibility	
Risk taking		Security		Service		Spirituality	
Stewardship		Teamwork		Trust		Wealth	
Wisdom							

My values: _____

_____

_____

_____

_____

_____

Begin the exercise by crossing off or marking ones that do not resonate with you. Keep crossing them off until you have five to seven personal values that are critical to who you are and to which you always abide. Be very honest with yourself; this exercise is for your eyes only. If you realize that you are not pleased with some of your current values (which are driving your behavior), select only those that make you feel good about yourself.

Write down your final list of values somewhere so that you can refer to them until they become part of you and they drive your decisions and actions.

Motivation

Human motivation is a complex construct. To simplify the idea, motivation boils down to two overarching drivers: unsatisfied needs (per Maslow) and fear.

Motivation drives behavior. If you are motivated to get an unsatisfied need met, your behavior will be directed toward need fulfillment. If you are motivated by fear, your behavior will be directed away from or against that fear. This idea is illustrated by Figure 1.2.

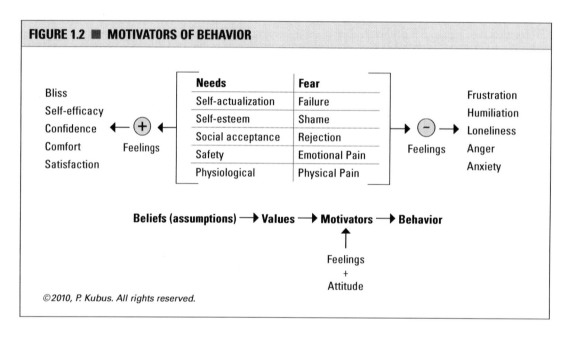

FIGURE 1.2 ■ MOTIVATORS OF BEHAVIOR

	Needs	Fear	
	Self-actualization	Failure	
	Self-esteem	Shame	
Bliss / Self-efficacy / Confidence / Comfort / Satisfaction ← (+) Feelings ←	Social acceptance	Rejection	→ (−) Feelings → Frustration / Humiliation / Loneliness / Anger / Anxiety
	Safety	Emotional Pain	
	Physiological	Physical Pain	

Beliefs (assumptions) → Values → Motivators → Behavior

↑

Feelings + Attitude

On the left side of the diagram, you see Maslow's hierarchy of needs. To get those needs satisfied, you will be motivated to take the actions necessary. For example, if you are a new nurse manager at a new hospital, one of your needs is to be accepted by your new peer group. Actions you might take to satisfy this need are:

- Setting up individual meetings with each of your new peers to get to know them

- Attending all service meetings with this group

- Seeking advice from them

- Offering your support to them

- Determining how you can help them

- Asking one of them to mentor you

- Attending social functions with this group

What you notice about this list is that all the activities are positive actions toward your goal of being accepted by your new peer group. Acceptance into this group will provide you with feelings of comfort, support, confidence, and camaraderie. These are all positive feelings and they resulted from your actions of moving toward getting a need fulfilled.

Look at the right side of the diagram: fear. Let's stay with the same example, only this time you didn't take any of the actions listed previously and your peers are feeling rejected by you and they stop including you in meetings or conversations. You are now feeling rejected, with accompanying feelings of loneliness and maybe even humiliation. If you are now operating from a fear motive (stress), your behaviors will be either fight (aggression) or, more likely, flight (withdrawal). You start operating on your own and avoiding the group, allowing the void to grow.

Feelings that are generated out of fear include:
- Frustration

- Anger

- Jealousy

- Shame

- Humiliation

- Greed

- Anxiety

- Loneliness

- Depression

- Somatic complaints

- Uselessness

The behaviors that are generated from fear will always be fight or flight, attacking or contracting. Some behaviors that result from these feelings include:

- **Fight:** verbal or physical aggression, theft, lying, gossiping, etc.

- **Flight:** withdrawal, escape, addiction, rumination, passive aggression, etc.

Unless you are trying to escape physical harm, these behaviors never lead to anything positive—such as getting your needs met. Their goal is to reduce the fear or pain in a very ineffective way.

> *"How very little can be done under the spirit of fear."*
> *—Florence Nightingale*

Here's one final point to consider about motivation: The positive feelings from getting needs met (joy, tranquility, optimism, satisfaction, confidence, self-efficacy, comfort, bliss) lead to positive behaviors for yourself and others. These behaviors include sharing, giving of yourself to others, trusting yourself and others, and caring for your-self and others. These are all expansive behaviors of abundance. These are the behaviors of authentic leaders.

Strengths and limitations

Everyone has some very specific strengths. You should be clear about what those strengths are and continue to build on them. If you are uncertain about some of them, ask others for some feedback.

There are also several behavioral inventories available that can help assist you in identifying your strengths:

- The Birkman Method® (*www.birkman.com*)
- DISC
- Hogan (*www.hoganassessments.com*)
- StrengthsFinder (*www.strengthsfinder.com*)

Some of these inventories require a certified consultant to help you interpret the results correctly. Your human resources (HR) department may be able to help you find someone who can administer and debrief these inventories for you. There also may be professionals in your HR department who are certified.

Another way to identify your strengths and limitations is to get feedback from those around you to verify your self-perceptions. One of your goals should be to focus on your strengths. Too often, we tend to focus on our limitations and forget that we should always be investing in our strengths. Continue to build on your strengths and use them to the fullest.

When you are using your strengths, life is much more exciting. When you are "in flow," you are fully engaged in an interesting activity and time passes quickly. Csikszentmihalyi (1997) puts it aptly in his book *Finding Flow*:

> *When goals are clear, feedback relevant, and challenges and skills are in balance, attention becomes ordered and fully invested. Because of the total demand on psychic energy, a person in flow is completely focused.*

Be aware of times when you are feeling as though you are in flow. What are you doing? It is likely that this activity will be challenging. The skills that are necessary to be good at this challenging activity are likely to be some of your strengths. If you are like most people, you will soon become bored doing tasks that are too easy for you.

CASE STUDY

Flow Scenario 1

Marianne, a pediatric service director, is "in flow" when coaching and developing her managers. She listens to Karen, the cardiac pediatric manager, share an experience about a difficult performance situation she is having with one of her staff. Marianne is competent at understanding human motivation and is able to ask Karen several questions that help her clarify the situation in her own mind. Marianne can guide Karen through several options on how best to confront the staff nurse. Together, they determine the best course of action. Marianne role-plays with Karen what she will say to the staff member. Karen leaves the discussion feeling competent in her own ability to confront the staff nurse.

Marianne's strengths: *listening, coaching, giving feedback, and empowering others.*

Weaknesses

We all have limitations (or weaknesses) and we need to be clear about what those are. Some limitations could really limit our careers, and steps might need to be taken to mitigate them if they are getting in the way of maximum effectiveness. Limitations are one of many reasons why it is important to have a diverse team to support you. It makes sense to have someone on your team who is really good in an area where you struggle.

Think about an example of two colleagues: one is visionary and strategic whereas the other is operational and detail-oriented. Their strengths are complementary and can be helpful to the other. Having someone on your team who is great in an area where you are not is like adding another lens to your camera.

Strengths/weaknesses identification

Figure 1.3 is a list of qualities that could be either strengths or weaknesses. Identify your top three strengths and your top three areas that need to be developed. Get some feedback from your colleagues, your direct reports, and your manager to verify your list. Alternatively, ask them to fill out this list and return it to you anonymously (if they feel more comfortable).

FIGURE 1.3 ■ PERSONAL VALUES EXERCISE

Quality	Strength	Weakness
Building strong relationships		
Change management		
Creative thinking		
Critical thinking		
Communication		
Coaching		
Confrontation		
Decision-making		
Delegation		
Detail orientation		
Developing others		
Emotional intelligence		
Execution		
Financial analysis		
Flexibility		
Influencing		
Learning		
Openness to new ideas		
Persuasion		
Planning and organizing		
Professional presence		
Reading the environment		
Self-awareness		
Strategic planning		
Teaching		
Technology		
Team building		
Writing		

To authentically lead others, self-awareness and self-acceptance are critical. You will be able to role model adherence to your values, you will know when you slip into fear behaviors, and you will humbly be open about your strengths as well as your weaknesses. You will know which path you need to take to continue to grow to meet the ever-changing demands of today's complex healthcare arena. You will be able to lead others, and they will be excited to join you on the journey.

"The world is put back by the death of everyone who has to sacrifice the development of his or her peculiar gifts to conventionality."
—*Florence Nightingale*

LEADERSHIP TIP

Bill George (2003), former CEO of Medtronic, lists five dimensions of authentic leaders. They:

1. **Understand their purpose:** This is the reason they move into leadership roles. Authentic leaders have a purpose to make a positive difference in the world by showing others the way and helping them reach their potential (Greenleaf, 2002).

2. **Practice solid values:** These define one's character and help to build trust with others.

3. **Lead with heart:** Demonstrate caring and compassion for others.

4. **Establish connected relationships:** This is a basic leadership competency. Great leaders admit they cannot do it alone.

5. **Demonstrate self-discipline:** Always adhere to values, which helps build trust (the foundation for any relationship).

Being authentic means that you are real and genuine. This helps others know they can trust you to do what is best for everyone, not just yourself, even when the going gets tough (which it always does.)

References

1. Csikszentmihalyi, M. (1997). *Finding Flow: The Psychology of Engagement with Everyday Life.* New York: Basic Books.

2. George, B. (2003). *Authentic Leadership: Rediscovering the Secrets to Creating Lasting Value.* San Francisco: Jossey-Bass.

3. George, B. (2007). *True North: Discover Your Authentic Leadership.* San Francisco: Jossey-Bass.

4. Greenleaf, R. K. (2002). *Servant Leadership: A Journey into the Nature of Legitimate Power and Greatness.* Mahwah, NJ: Paulist Press.

5. Covey, S. R. (1990). *The 7 Habits of Highly Effective People.* New York: Free Press.

6. Covey, S. R. (1994). *First Things First.* New York: Fireside.

ORGANIZATIONAL CULTURE

Learning Objectives

After reading this chapter, the reader will be able to:

- Define organizational culture

- List the three general types of organizational cultures

- Describe how the culture is communicated and embedded in the organization

Of all the elements that affect human behavior, *organizational culture* is the primary determinant of how people act in the workplace. This is why understanding your culture is so important. If you want or need to change people's behavior, look at the culture because that is what is driving employees' actions.

Culture is an intangible concept, which can be difficult to describe. This means it can be overlooked when you're trying to effect change or diagnose a problem. If you break culture down into its elements, it becomes manageable and modifications can be made that would initiate and sustain a change in behavior of the constituents who make up the culture.

You and your staff are faced with changes every day. Understanding how the culture operates can help or hinder your staff's agility to make the ever-increasing rate of change tolerable. They may even come to embrace it.

> **LEADERSHIP TIP**
>
> Having a unit culture that emphasizes participative decision-making, open communication, and teamwork has been shown to be positively related to commitment, empowerment, job satisfaction, and nurses intent to stay (Gifford, Zammuto & Goodman, 2002).

Understanding Organizational Culture

The concept of culture, which originated in the anthropological domain, has various definitions. Fertig (1996) defines culture as a way of life of a group of people who share a feeling of common identity and through which people adapt to their social and physical environments. Notice the word *adapt*. Organizations must constantly determine how to adapt to changing environments, and the culture is the medium through which adaptation occurs and is sustained. Survival and success go to the agile organizations that are able to identify the values and practices that should stay and those that must be altered.

Culture can also be defined as a pattern of *shared* basic assumptions (which are the foundation of values) that a group learns and that is taught to new members so they know the proper way to perceive, think, feel, and behave (Schein, 1992). Deal and Kennedy (1982) define it as "the way we do things around here." If you're comfortable with "the way things are done here," that's great. However, if there are some things that could be done differently to improve effectiveness—such as communication, quality, safety, service, etc.—then you need to look at the culture that is currently supporting the present behaviors.

The concept of culture becomes much clearer when it is broken down into the elements that compose it:

- **Assumptions.** Assumptions are deeply held beliefs that we rarely think about or discuss (Schein, 1992). We hold assumptions about people and relationships: Are their intentions typically good or evil? Are they industrious or lazy? Are people out for their own gain or are they collaborative? Does everyone have an equal chance at success? We also make assumptions about resources: Are they scarce or abundant? We hold assumptions at a deep, usually unconscious, level.

- **Values.** Values can be thought of as principles that are positive and that drive behavior because of their importance to the organization. Core values should be determined and agreed to by representatives from all parts of an organization and must be role-modeled by the leadership team. Organizational values should be easily found on every website and may include examples such as quality patient care, customer focus, teamwork, embracing change, diversity, respect, research leadership, education, etc.

- **Leaders.** At the foundation of any culture are the founders of the organization and the leaders who are presently in place. You shape the culture (and thus the behavior) by what you do and what you pay attention to. You are constantly communicating, and constantly role modeling, whether you realize it or not, and thus you must be constantly vigilant that your actions are in line with the espoused values. People will always believe your actions over your words. Employees are acutely aware of how you act, especially during times of celebration and crisis (Schein, 1992). As a leader, you create and define meaning for both internal and external constituents. People look to you to help them understand the implications of what is going on in their internal, as well as external, environments, for example: leadership changes, reorganizations, MRSA outbreaks, the current economic state, the flu pandemic, healthcare reform, practice changes, etc.

- **External environment.** Included in the external environment are patients, benefactors, the economy, new legislation, societal expectations, political forces, the community, and competition. Any of these factors can create a shift in the practices or policies and thereby create changes in the culture.

- **Employees.** Just as you are affected by the external environment, so are employees. Employees also affect the culture through their collaboration with and input to you, their leader. Today, we are seeing the differences in the many generations in the workplace and noticing how different Generations X and Y are from the baby boomers and veteran generations in terms of how they work and the expectations they set for themselves and their employers. The new generations bring their influence to the culture of any organization.

Those are the elements or building blocks of any organization's culture. It is a dynamic system with all parts interacting with and affecting the others.

Importance of understanding your culture

Understanding organizational culture is a competency nurse leaders must develop, since it is the role of leadership to grow the organization and its people in response to the changing external environment. Leadership is about creating sustainable change. Sustainable change is required for growth, which is necessary for life. Nothing stands still unless it's dead or dying. Think of a muscle; it needs a balance of work and rest or it will atrophy. If it isn't stretched, it will get tight and inflexible to the demands of the environment. In the same way, organizations need to be agile so they can respond quickly, and it's the culture that determines how adaptive the organization really is.

If you want to understand how to develop your staff for a higher level of functioning— one that is self-actualized and adaptive—you need to understand your culture to ensure that the culture actually supports what you are trying to do. What you as the leader do and the processes you create will either support that goal or thwart it.

Here's an example to illustrate the point. Imagine you tell your staff that you want them to work better as a team. You offer some team-building programs and feel that you have given them the tools they need, but you notice there is little demonstration of the teamwork principles you know they just learned and you wonder why. To find the answer, you need to look at the culture to determine where the block is. Start by looking at yourself. What are you role modeling? Next, look at the processes and procedures to see what is in the way. Have you put anything in place to support teamwork? Have you removed barriers to teamwork? Then, look at rewards and incentives. Are people being rewarded for teamwork or for individual work?

> *"Culture isn't just one aspect of the game, it is the game."*
> —*Gerstner, 2002*

How culture is manifested

Next, let's look at how a culture is manifested and sustained. There are several things to consider:

- **Role modeling.** By serving as role models, leaders communicate what is important, how to succeed, how to behave, and even how to speak and dress. It is absolutely critical that you walk the talk to build and maintain a strong culture. Without consistent modeling, followers are left in a state of confusion, wondering what it is they are supposed to do to succeed and be accepted by the group. Leaders personify the values of the culture (Deal & Kennedy, 1982). Role modeling is the most effective way to embed the values of a culture into the organization. Your staff will pay attention to what is important to you, what you measure, what you communicate, and what you do. You are always communicating, whether you are thinking about it or not, so be aware of your behavior.

- **Socialization process.** New members acquire the norms of behavior through the socialization process with existing members (Schein, 1992). Although some of the culture is transmitted formally through presentations from top leadership and written materials, most is transmitted informally through peers and observation. Nurses who are new to your hospital or unit typically get a preceptor assigned to them. The new nurse will carefully watch everything the preceptor

Chapter 2

does and the effects of those behaviors, and will begin to adopt the behaviors of the preceptor. It can be helpful to assign new nurses a mentor. Mentors support people as they attempt to develop to their fullest and learn ways to navigate the political landscape of the organization. Mentors can be extremely helpful both to organizational newcomers and to nurses who have been identified as "high potential" or who have been promoted into a new role. Without a mentor, newcomers can struggle for months while trying to identify the code of behavior in the new organization or in the new role, leaving them stressed and fatigued.

- **Structures and processes.** Structure refers to two things. One is the physical building, which might be modern or more traditional and homey. The appearance of the building will tell you something about the culture. Secondly, structure refers to the organizational chart or hierarchy. Is it flat or top-heavy with lots of supporting bureaucracy? Will there be advancement opportunities for you? How easy will it be for you to get a question answered or obtain a resource? You can start to determine some of these questions by observing the structure. The systems, processes, and procedures also give an indication of the culture. Look at the following systems, processes, and procedures: decision-making, hiring, firing, promoting, communication (how and to whom), resource allocation, training and development, strategic planning, and conflict resolution. Are they nimble or cumbersome processes? Does everyone have access? Are representatives from various departments and levels represented in big decisions? How long do these processes take? Are decisions frequently made in crisis mode or is there a defined, succinct, planned process? Are they fair?

- **Artifacts.** Artifacts include rituals, celebrations, symbols, stories, and various objects that help to embed the culture. They are things you can see or hear. An example of a ritual is morning report, an example of a celebration is National Nurses Week festivities or a retirement party, and a symbol could be a lapel pin or stethoscope around your neck. Stories told about particularly memorable events embed the culture by reinforcing values and drawing the group together.

20   **Lead! Becoming an Effective Coach and Mentor to Your Nursing Staff**
© 2010 HCPro, Inc.

Figure 2.1 is a concept map that details how each of the elements relates to the others.

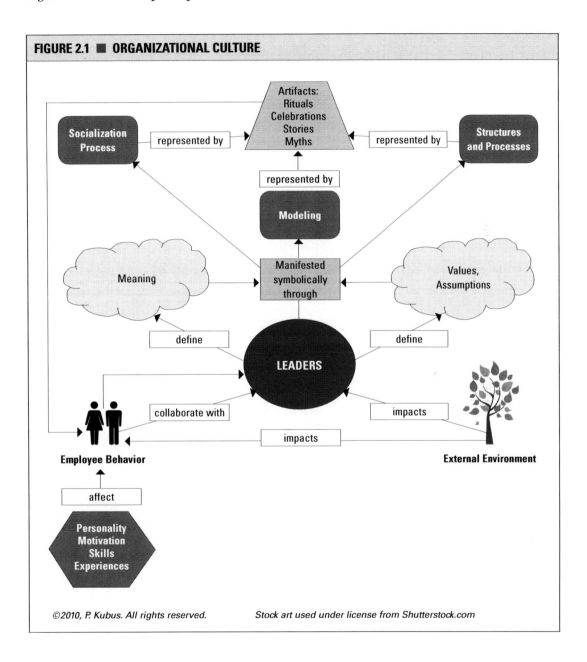

FIGURE 2.1 ■ ORGANIZATIONAL CULTURE

©2010, P. Kubus. All rights reserved.   Stock art used under license from Shutterstock.com

Types of Organizational Culture

To understand your organization's culture, it can be worthwhile to examine what type it falls into. There are several organizational culture inventories available. One that is widely used is the *Organizational Culture Inventory* (Cooke & Lafferty, 1994), which breaks culture down into three types (Cooke & Szumal, 1993): constructive, passive-defensive, and aggressive-defensive.

Constructive culture

A constructive culture is defined as one that is achievement oriented and encourages members to interact with each other in a manner that supports members to reach their self-actualized needs and group goals. Terms used to describe this type of culture include: innovative, empathetic, challenging, collaborative, supportive of professional development, considerate of others, accomplishment/goal-focused, respectful, and risk-taking.

Passive–defensive culture

A passive–defensive culture can be described as one where members interact in a way that protects their own security. Terms to describe this type of culture include: group acceptance, agreeable, risk avoidant, not challenging the status quo, absence of independent action, and absence of taking ideas forward.

Aggressive-defensive culture

An aggressive-defensive culture is one where members are focused on their own tasks and competing with each other to get ahead. Descriptors of this type of culture include: competitive, critical of others, change resistant, detached, micromanaging, perfectic, and political.

Keep in mind, all cultures have some elements from each of these types, but there is usually a dominant pattern that is fairly obvious. That dominant pattern will drive member behavior.

You need to know the dominant pattern for your organization and unit to see whether it is the best type of culture for your situation. If you have an aggressive-defensive culture (see previous descriptors) but need a constructive culture because change is coming fast, you need to look at what is driving the current culture (which isn't the one you need) and fix it. Although you, as a manager, won't be able to change the culture of the entire organization—since that must come from top leadership—you *can* change the culture on your unit.

Culture Identification

How would you describe the culture of your organization? To get a precise read on the culture of a specific organization, a reasonably thorough analysis would be required using either an organizational culture inventory and/or a series of structured focus groups led by an outsider with extensive knowledge about culture (Schein, 1999). A place to begin your own analysis would be by looking at the elements:

- Values—What are the espoused values? Where did they come from?

- Leader—What does he or she do? Which of the previous descriptors most close-ly matches his or her/your behavior?

- Artifacts—What is the history of the artifacts? Why have they perpetuated?

- Structures and processes—Which of the three types of culture listed previously best describe your structures and processes?

- Socialization process—Is there one? What type of information is reviewed in orientation and on-boarding? Is what is described actually in sync with practice?

Reflecting on these questions will begin to bring into focus your organization's culture. You will need to be able to describe it when you are interviewing candidates that you are considering hiring. They need to know what the culture is like at your hospital, and you need to determine if they will be a good fit for your culture.

Think about how uncomfortable the following scenario would be for a newcomer to your hospital. Candidate A is coming from an institution that has a very bureaucratic culture that included the elements of the aggressive-defensive culture described earlier in this chapter. Candidate A is used to hoarding information and power, competing with others to always be right, not trusting too many colleagues, never speaking up to offer ideas or challenge the process, and never taking risks. Candidate A might like the culture or she might not, but it's a way of behaving that she knows.

However, in this example, your culture is more constructive and self-actualizing. People openly offer ideas and disagree so that the best solution can be created, knowledge and power are shared, and collaboration and trust is rampant. This candidate needs to know this information before deciding whether to accept the position. Suppose she came to your hospital and behaved as if she were at her last place of employment? She would neither thrive nor do well. She would need explicit guidance on how to behave in the new culture in order to be accepted and excel. That's why you need to be able to describe your culture.

Strong vs. weak cultures

Strong cultures will influence behavior more than will weak cultures. This is good if the culture is the correct type of culture for the organization's needs based on where it wants to go given the external environment. A strong culture is one where everyone understands the culture and behaves in a way that is consistent with it. In other words, if you ask several people to describe the culture and you get similar answers, you likely have a strong culture (the values are widely shared). Conversely, if their answers are very different, you likely have a weak culture and behavior will be inconsistent.

Subcultures

Although the culture of the organization is set by the top leadership, you will have influence over the subculture of your nursing organization, service, or unit. Although it will be challenging to create a subculture that is vastly different from the one that your executives have created, you can create some variations to make the culture in your organization more effective for you and your team.

Why is it important to understand culture?

Culture determines how people behave. Leaders are a primary determinant of the culture. Therefore, if you want to create a coaching culture, you need to role model coaching behaviors, set up a socialization process that communicates the importance of feedback and coaching, and you need to establish a process for feedback and coaching. The types of leader behavior that lead to a constructive organizational culture include ones that are mission, vision, and value focused; supportive and encouraging in helping others develop their skills; confident in their own skills and aware of shortcomings; creative; optimistic about the future; flexible; and open and honest in communication.

If you are not seeing the types of behaviors you would like to see from your staff, examine the culture. Make changes in your behavior, as well as in the structures, processes, and procedures so all are aligned with the culture that best supports the behaviors you want to see demonstrated every day.

References

1. Cooke, R. A., & Lafferty, J. C. (1994). *Organizational Culture Inventory.* Plymouth, MI: Human Synergistics.

2. Cooke, R. A., & Szumal, J. L. (1993). "Measuring normative beliefs and shared behavioral expectations in organizations: The reliability and validity of the organizational culture inventory." *Psychological Reports*, 72, 1299–1330.

3. Deal, T. E., & Kennedy, A. A. (1982). *Corporate Cultures: The Rites and Rituals of Corporate Life.* Reading, MA: Perseus Books.

4. Gerstner, L. V., Jr. (2002). *Who Says Elephants Can't Dance?* New York: Harper Collins.

5. Gifford, B. D., Zammuto, R. F., & Goodman, E. A. (2002). "The relationship between hospital unit culture and nurses' quality of work life." *Journal of Healthcare Management*, 47(1), 13–26.

6. Fertig, G. (1996). Investigating the process of cultural change from an anthropological perspective. *Social Studies, 87*(4), 165–171.

7. Schein, E. H. (1992). *Organizational Culture and Leadership.* San Francisco: Jossey-Bass.

8. Schein, E. H. (1999). *The Corporate Culture Survival Guide.* San Francisco: Jossey-Bass.

CHAPTER 3

THE IMPORTANCE OF TRUST

Learning Objectives

After reading this chapter, the reader will be able to:

- ■ Explain why trust is essential for authentic leaders
- ■ Describe ways to build trusting relationships

Trusting relationships are important to you as a leader for many reasons. Trust is necessary for success, whether it is self-trust in relation to your personal goal achievement or in your organization for the realization of the goals you, collectively, have agreed are necessary for organizational survival and growth.

You have to trust your colleagues, leaders, and staff to perform their jobs in a manner that supports organizational values and helps to move the organization toward its vision.

What Is Trust?

Trust is having confidence in yourself, another person, a system, or a process that the agreed-upon behavior and anticipated outcome will occur. Trust is a comforting feeling that your expectations will be met:

- • I trust myself to keep promises to myself.

- I trust you to tell me the truth.

- I trust that the system will work.

- I trust the process. I will not deviate from it.

"Self-trust is the first secret of success."
—*Ralph Waldo Emerson*

Consider how comforting and freeing it is to trust yourself. Goals that you set for yourself bring with them a series of tasks or events necessary for the accomplishment of that goal. For example:

- Running a marathon

- Taking a class

- Teaching a class

- Learning a new skill

- Getting a master's degree

Occasionally, people set lofty goals but become weary as they take the first steps or as they hit the first wall of resistance. Trusting yourself means that you know you will not give up when obstacles come your way, doors close, or weariness sets in. Authentic leaders trust themselves to persevere to the finish line. They know they will do what it takes for successful completion. Trusting yourself saves a lot of time and frustration and will help you build trusting relationships with others as you become trustworthy.

Likewise, trusting relationships with others make life easier, more enjoyable, and rewarding. You don't have to continually second-guess their motives and check up on them to be sure they are telling you the truth. When you seek their input, you know they will give you honest feedback and share ideas that are in your best interest. When they appear to slight you, you give them the benefit of the doubt, and you don't waste a lot of emotional energy feeling either hurt or trying to figure out their motives. Feedback can flow back and forth freely for the benefit of each person and for the enrichment of the relationship.

A good metaphor for the process of building trust is the process of constructing a building. The depth of the foundation (trust) is determined by the size of the structure (a toolshed or a high rise). The largest buildings (for example, the Empire State Building) will require the deepest and strongest foundation. The largest buildings are like your most important relationships: in your personal life, that is with your significant other or person you marry; in your professional life, it includes relationships with your direct reports, your peers, and the leadership team above you. A well-built foundation will sustain the relationship from the elements that will batter it over the years. Strong foundations take planning, effort, time, and quality raw materials. If you use faulty steel and porous concrete, no amount of planning, effort, and time will compensate. Therefore, be sure the person you are considering entering into a trusting relationship with is trustworthy and has the character, skills, and motivations for the role.

LEADERSHIP TIP

Creating a culture of trust requires authentic leaders.

Trust saves time and money, and reduces stress

The thesis of Stephen M. R. Covey's *The Speed of Trust* (2006) is that when trust is present, people can move faster, saving time and money. When you trust others, you can take their word to be true; they will do what they say they will do. You can put their word in the bank.

If your manager says he or she will support your growth and development and will always be there if your footing starts to get shaky or if you lose direction, you will operate in a confident manner where you feel comfortable taking risks. You can walk a tightrope with some confidence, because you know there is a net below you. Getting to the other side will be an exhilarating experience since the task was challenging, you used new skills, and you had support. Everyone wins and your performance and confidence are taken to a new level. Your likelihood of taking another risk and pushing your skills further is great.

If, however, there were no net, think about how slowly and frightfully you would traverse the abyss below you, if you would try to make it across at all. Every muscle in your body would be tense, you would feel enormous stress, and fatigue would follow. You would move across very slowly, tentatively, and with great trepidation. Would you feel exhilarated after crossing the abyss? Most likely, you would feel not only some sense of relief but also possibly some anger when you consider the consequences of the tiniest misstep.

How often do people feel this way in the workplace when they are asked to do things when they feel neither confident nor supported and when the risk of failure is devastating, at least to their egos and self-esteem? Sadly, all too often. When you are scared and operating out of fear, your ability to use your brain slows as you prepare for fight or flight. It is exhausting. Getting through a situation such as this does not leave you feeling confident, triumphant, and excited about another, similar risk. It leaves you feeling depleted.

CASE STUDY

A recently promoted nurse manager, Cheryl, has the reputation of "walking on water." As a staff nurse, she was outstanding, clinically superb, and dedicated to her patients. The service director and executive staff are thrilled to see her in a management role.

Cheryl asks one of her staff members, Andrea, who is also somewhat new in her role, to participate in a challenging project. Cheryl feels that Andrea has the skills to excel at this project and offers her support through its execution. At one point in the project, Andrea is required to make a presentation to the CEO and a few others on the executive team about the status of the project. Cheryl is present at the presentation. When the CEO asks Andrea some questions that she can't answer, the CEO explodes and berates Andrea for her lack of knowledge and apparent incompetence. Instead of intervening and supporting Andrea, Cheryl sits quietly. She does not provide a net for Andrea. Cheryl lets Andrea take the heat alone.

Months later, when Andrea is asked to provide another update to the entire nursing leadership team, Andrea asks Cheryl for her input and for some coaching on the presentation. Cheryl makes an appointment with Andrea to review it, but Cheryl cancels the meeting at the last minute. Andrea pursues and tries to make another appointment. After Andrea makes several attempts to talk with her, Cheryl finally agrees to meet with Andrea 10 minutes before the presentation is about to start. It's too late. Andrea is forced to go into the meeting and make the presentation without a net once again. Trust in Cheryl is gone and after a few months, Andrea resigns.

When there is trust, you can act more quickly, saving time, resources, and stress.

Trust is necessary for:

- **Collaboration.** A foundation of trust also leads to active listening and dialogue, which are requirements for collaboration (Conger, 1992; Kouzes & Posner, 2002). If you don't trust someone, it is unlikely that you will really listen to the person and his or her ideas. It's like he or she is "not at the table." There is no dialogue and therefore, there can be no collaboration. It is common knowledge that collaboration leads to shared goals, effectiveness, and successful performance. If there's no trust, there's no collaboration. Trust is at the heart of collaboration (Annison & Wilford, 1998; Kouzes & Posner, 2002).

- **Effective change.** It is difficult to get someone to follow you on a new path, and perhaps cross an abyss, if he or she doesn't trust you. Would you follow someone down a dark alley if you had not built a trusting relationship with him or her? Unlikely. However, gazing at the same alley, if someone you respected and trusted asked you to follow him or her into the unknown because there would be rewards at the other end or because pain would be avoided if you moved from where you were, you would be more inclined to go. Coaching someone to try a new behavior will be much easier if he or she trusts you. The person will be confident that your guidance will be in his or her best interest and that he or she will not be harmed.

- **Empowerment.** Trusting, mutually respectful relationships are necessary to empower others to act (George, 2007). Powerful leaders give power away. When people feel powerful (as opposed to powerless), their level of engagement soars. They take responsibility, initiative, and risks. After coaching, feedback, and observation, leaders can trust staff to make the right decision and do the right thing. Staff members need to trust that leaders believe they have the skills for the task. Sharing power is a behavior of an authentic leader who knows that power is not a zero-sum game, but is actually quite the reverse.

- **Risk-taking.** Without taking risks and moving out of their comfort zones, neither organizations nor individuals move forward, grow, and flourish. Trust is an antecedent to risk-taking. Who is going to offer a differing point of view, give feedback to colleagues or managers, and try something new with the inherent possibility of failure, if reprisal is certain? Differing opinions and ideas, critical but loving feedback, mistakes, and healthy conflict are part of achieving great results (Lencioni, 2002). In fact, they are a requirement of success. The

Lead! Becoming an Effective Coach and Mentor to Your Nursing Staff

© 2010 HCPro, Inc.

safety of clinging to the status quo is not. The environment must have a foundation of trust before you or your staff will be willing to challenge the system in order to realize growth and success.

- **Influence.** One way to influence others is by listening to them and thereby being open to being influenced by them (Kouzes & Posner, 2002). This is a behavior by which leaders can demonstrate their trust in others and the value in their experience, skills, and abilities. Through role-modeling trust, you will begin to establish a trusting relationship so that when you need to influence others, they will be open to being influenced by you.

"Never underestimate the power of trust and its enduring effect on nurse leaders' success."
—Fitzpatrick, 2001

How to Build Trust

As discussed earlier in the chapter, building trust takes planning, effort, time, and quality raw materials. If you are a newcomer to an organization or role, take some time to reflect and plan how you will build a foundation of trust with those around you. Identify the people with whom an "Empire State Building" type of foundation will need to be created. Then think about which of the following tactics you should employ with each and how you will do it:

- Be trustworthy.

- Achieve competence in the skills needed for success in your role (reflect back on the strengths and weaknesses you identified in Chapter 1). You'll have a hard time getting people to trust you if you have not developed competency in your job. If you are new in your position, be honest about what skills you bring to the job, what skills you still are developing, and what your plan for development includes.

- Create a climate of open communication. Share as much information as you can (as appropriate) with others, including:

  - How you will support the organization's values

  - Your vision for your organization

  - Your ideas, thoughts, opinions; also ask for theirs

  - Asking for feedback and offering to give feedback

  - Listening to others with an open mind and expressing appreciation

- Treat others with respect.

- Keep your commitments and confidences.

- Support the development of others (give them the chance to grow *and* give them the net).

- Show value for diversity and divergent ideas.

- Recognize accomplishments and contributions; also express appreciation.

- Make your expectations explicit. You've heard Robert Frost's line "good fences make good neighbors." Your staff needs to know their boundaries and what you expect of them. Likewise, you should know their expectations of you. Agreement on expectations builds trust.

- Verify your assumptions. We make assumptions all the time about people, about events. If you feel that trust has possibly been breached by someone whom you trust, instead of making an assumption about what happened and letting a crack in the trust foundation form, check it out with him or her.

- Confront issues, not people.

- Avoid micromanagement; watching every detail of someone's work demonstrates distrust.

- Walk your talk; if what you do differs from what you say, people will always believe your actions. Keep them in sync.

How to Sustain Trust

Sustaining a trusting relationship requires vigilance and continued care and feeding. The way to sustain trust is to keep doing the action steps listed previously. Pay particular attention to the "Empire State Building" relationships. Sometimes, as you get comfortable over time, you can get complacent and forget to continue to put effort into the relationship.

Make a plan to continue to enhance your skills; learning and growing never stops. Even if you have a "terminal" degree, keep a plan for learning by attending conferences, networking with others in your field, taking classes, teaching classes, attending workshops, or getting some coaching.

Another thing that can slip over time is asking for feedback. Consider doing a 360-degree review on yourself every other year. A 360-degree review is a survey designed to get feedback from people all around you: your manager, your direct reports, your peers, your internal colleagues, etc. It will ask them questions about how effective you are in the various competencies needed to excel in your role, such as communication, planning, staff development, coaching, delegation, strategic planning, building relationships, influencing, etc.

A 360-degree review is designed only for development, not evaluation. It should never be used as an evaluation tool. The responses from your respondents are 100% anonymous; be sure this is part of your communication process. Your human resources department or coach can help you arrange this.

Remember to continue to recognize specific accomplishments and contributions. It is very motivating when your efforts are recognized and appreciated. Doing this once for someone is great, but it needs to happen on a regular basis as warranted. Public recognition is the best; be sure that you are fair and balanced in that you do this for everyone as the opportunity arises. If the opportunity doesn't arise for someone in particular, make it happen (provide him or her the opportunity) so that everyone gets some recognition for something. More on recognition will be presented in Chapter 13.

How to Repair Trust

In many situations where trust is breached, withdrawal is the typical response. The relationship ends or takes on a new cool air with the involved parties barely speaking, if at all. Most people are afraid to confront the other person, so they just pull away, and never trust that person again. However, trusting relationships can be repaired, most of the time. Of course, if sociopathic and psychopathic personalities are involved, there will be trouble building trusting relationships with anyone. However, that is not the case in most instances. Most of the time, trust can be rebuilt.

Everyone has been lied to or cheated at some point in their workplace. Sometimes it was intentional; many times it was not. Take a minute and reflect on a time when someone at your hospital violated your trust (see Figure 3.1).

Initially, when trust is breached, it is as if an emotional "punch in the stomach" is rendered. If the violation is both egregious *and* involves an "Empire State Building" level of relationship, the effect is literally a physical sensation. You have been assaulted and your system goes into fight or flight mode. The shock of the transgression can literally knock you off your feet. In the workplace, although this level of betrayal sometimes happens, most of the time trust betrayals are more moderate in scale. Regardless of the severity, there is frequently some type of visceral reaction to the transgression. You can feel it, and it doesn't feel good.

FIGURE 3.1 ■ REBUILDING TRUST

Think about someone who breached trust with you. Describe:

1. What they did:

_____

_____

2. How you felt:

_____

_____

3. What you did:

_____

_____

4. How the relationship changed:

_____

_____

The main reason that trust is breached is fear. This can include:

- Fear of repercussion or retaliation: To prevent someone from getting angry or hurt, people lie.

- Fear of failure: When things move too fast and when there are multiple pressures/stressors being exerted, it becomes a survival mechanism to focus only on the self. People don't always stop and think about all the repercussions that their actions will have on others. (Lack of maturity also keeps people self-absorbed.) Some people will do or say anything to avoid the humiliation of having to admit they don't know it all or that they made a mistake.

- Fear of not having enough: This fear leads to greed (lying, cheating, and stealing), which means that others have to go without.

This trust-breaking behavior can come in the form of disclosure of confidential information; not keeping a commitment; not telling the entire truth; blatant lying, cheating, and stealing; sabotaging others; gossip; making an assumption and acting on it; or sidestepping challenging issues.

The good news is that most of the time these trust-betraying behaviors are not intentional. People really can get too busy and focused on the task at hand that they can overlook the big picture, which includes you and others. In these types of situations, trust will be easily repaired assuming both parties are willing to discuss the transgression and move on. However, in situations when the transgression is not intentional but the effect is great, it may be a long rebuilding process. Think of an example when a group of employees *hears* a vice president (VP) say that there will be no layoffs, and four months after, they are told there will be layoffs and given a list of names. When the stakes of your communication are high, be excruciatingly careful about your choice of words. In this case, the VP claimed never to have said that there would not be layoffs, but still, that is what employees heard. You can imagine that this would be a long trust-rebuilding process since the foundation was shaken.

You now need to rebuild the emotional bank account as Covey (1989) calls it. This means that the transgressor needs to take steps to repair the relationship and the transgressee needs to keep track of the rebuilding efforts made so that both can move forward in what *can be* an even stronger relationship.

Take the following steps to rebuild the foundation of trust:

1. Acknowledge the transgression

2. Take responsibility

3. Air feelings

4. Apologize

5. Ask for forgiveness

6. Make amends

7. Create an agreement for the future

8. Keep track of efforts

If you were the person who was, for example, lied to, you need to take responsibility and start the process discussed earlier by confronting the person who lied to you. Confront him or her in a gentle manner since this person might not be aware he or she did not tell you the truth, in which case you made an assumption. If this person is aware, he or she may need coaching from you about the process listed previously. It is unlikely that the person is a sociopath or psychopath, in which case he or she will not take responsibility, apologize, forgive, etc. If so, this person will never be trustworthy and it's good that you know that. However, most rational, mature people will admit their fear and mistakes and will agree to a plan to repair and move forward.

> *"The root cause of most failed personal and business relationships is the inability to build, maintain and recover trust."*
> —*Boutros & Joseph, 2007*

Are People Generally Trustworthy?

Think of it like a normal bell curve, as in Figure 3.2. There will be a few people whom you can trust with everything, and there will be a few people whom you will never be able to trust with anything. Most people are somewhere in between. When you enter a new relationship with someone, think of that person as starting from the middle of the curve. Then as he or she either builds your trust (and you his or hers) or violates your trust, the person's position on the graph changes. When trust is breached, and his or her position on the graph shifts to the left, a bell should go off in your head that the foundation needs to be repaired. You should take responsibility to take the first step toward reparation. There are many occasions when

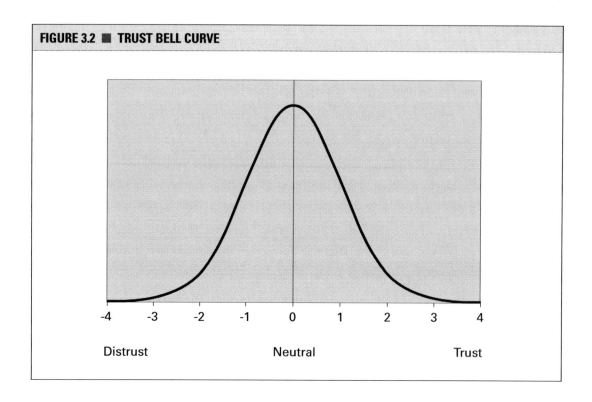

FIGURE 3.2 ■ TRUST BELL CURVE

a damaged relationship can be restored to a level that is even better than before trust was broken. After the parties involved dig deep and really work at repairing the damage, a stronger bond can end up being formed.

It is critical to build and, if needed, rebuild trusting relationships so that everyone can enjoy job satisfaction, growth, and success. You are responsible for every relationship that you enter: for building, maintaining, and rebuilding trust so that your relationships have foundations of integrity.

References

1. Annison, M. H., & Wilford, D. S. (1998). *Trust Matters: New Directions in Health Care Leadership*. San Francisco: Jossey-Bass.

2. Boutros, A., & Joseph, C. B. (2007). "Building, maintaining and recovering trust: A core leadership competency." *The Physician Executive*, 33(1), 38–41.

3. Conger, J. A. (1992). *Learning to Lead: The Art of Transforming Managers into Leaders*. San Francisco: Jossey-Bass.

4. Covey, S. M. R. (2006). *The Speed of Trust*. New York: Free Press.

5. Covey, S. R., (1989). *The 7 Habits of Highly Effective People*. New York: Fireside.

6. Fitzpatrick, M. A. (2001). "Famous last words: Trust me." *Nursing Management*, 32(6), 6.

7. George, B. (2007). *True North: Discover Your Authentic Leadership*. San Francisco: Jossey-Bass.

8. Kouzes, J. M. & Posner, B. Z. (2002). *The Leadership Challenge* (3rd ed.). San Francisco: Jossey-Bass.

9. Lencioni, P. M. (2002). *The Five Dysfunctions of a Team: A Leadership Fable*. San Francisco: Jossey-Bass.

HIRING THE BEST

Learning Objectives

After reading this chapter, the reader will be able to:

■ State the steps of a sound interview process

■ Describe the benefits of hiring the best

Nursing leaders make many decisions. One of the most important decisions any manager makes is whom they hire (or promote.) Hiring/promoting the best talent makes your job much more rewarding and enjoyable, but also easier. Consider yourself the gatekeeper of your culture. You, as the hiring manager, determine who gets in, who gets access to power and advancement, and who must leave.

Your hiring decision can have four possible results. You can:

1. Hire a great nurse

2. Hire an under-qualified nurse

3. Reject a great nurse

4. Reject an under-qualified nurse

The best decision is, of course, to hire a great nurse who is technically sharp, is motivated to care for patients, and has great interpersonal skills to work with the rest of the team, patients, and their families. Another good decision is to reject the under-qualified nurse. Both of the remaining two possibilities represent a bad decision: hire an under-qualified nurse and reject a great nurse. Which decision is worse? If you chose "hire the under-qualified nurse" you would be correct. Your selection decisions have a huge effect on your team, on you, on your performance and reputation, on your colleagues and partners, and on the organization. Select great talent, and everyone wins. Select poorly, and everyone loses.

LEADERSHIP TIP

In times of nursing shortages, there is the temptation to hire a warm body out of desperation, only to find that the time and energy required either to bring that person up to speed or to work them out of the system is both exhaustive and exhausting. It ends up doing a disservice to them and also to you, your staff, and the organization. It becomes a costly mistake, financially and emotionally.

A rule of thumb is that any hiring mistake costs the organization approximately twice the person's annual salary. The cost of the emotional stress and strain on you, your new hire, and your staff cannot be calculated.

Looking at the Big Picture

You are an integral part of the talent selection process. It is best to have a clear understanding of the broader context prior to beginning the interview process. One thing you want to consider is why you have an opening. Is it due to turnover, or did you just expand your service area and are presently in a growth period? If the vacancy is due to turnover, was it voluntary (the person left for a new position or for personal reasons) or was it involuntary (they were terminated for poor performance or a violation of policy). Think about the reasons for the vacancy so that you don't repeat a mistake, if that applies.

Is all turnover a bad thing? Although you don't want to lose great nurses, new people can bring fresh ideas, perspectives, knowledge, and skills to your unit even if they come from other units at your hospital. Work with your human resources (HR) department to answer the following questions:

- What is the turnover rate on my unit, in my service, and in my hospital? Look at how your unit compares to other areas. Is the turnover rate on your unit higher or lower than that of your service and hospital? Is it *much* higher or lower? Think about why this is so. If you don't know, ask others: your manager, your staff, and your HR department. If there is an exit interview process (and there should be), the HR department will be able to share that data with you. Finding answers to these questions will help you:

  - Improve situations that may be causing nurses to leave

  - Ensure that the reasons are out of your control (demographic shifts, economic shifts, the closing of a local business, etc.)

- What is the ratio of voluntary to involuntary (termination) turnover? Again, look at how this compares to other areas. If your area has a high percentage of involuntary turnovers, meaning that you have had to fire more staff than other areas, investigate the reason for that. You might discover that there is a particular person or process on your unit that is the cause for the turnover. Alternatively, it could be an inadequate selection system.

- What is the reputation of the hospital, of your service, and of your unit? Why is that so?

- How big is the typical applicant pool for an opening on your unit? This will determine just how selective you can be or whether you might have to wait until you find the right candidate.

- How does your nurse recruiter find and then prequalify candidates before they come to you? Know what the recruiter reviews and the cut-off scores that will drop candidates from the process versus move them forward, which could include:

© 2010 HCPro, Inc.

- Résumé: previous experience, how many years, where, what type of unit

- Transcripts, grade point average, honors, awards, school

- License

- Certifications

- Preemployment testing (aptitude, knowledge, motivation, organizational fit)

Know Whom You Are Looking for: Blueprint of the Best Candidate

What does it take to be successful on your unit? You probably already know this, but if not, be sure that you have a clear picture of whom you seek. It is likely that your HR department has carefully determined the competencies and qualifications of the successful person for the role under consideration, but they may not know the intricacies of each unit. Talk with your HR department to ensure they have a good understanding of the open position.

Performance is based ability, motivation, opportunity, and culture.

Ability

Consider the knowledge, competencies, and experience required for successful performance on your unit. You will gather data on knowledge and experience from the résumé. Competencies are "characteristics of employees with behavioral implications that are thought to be associated with successful performance of their job" (Garman & Johnson, 2006). You can gather this information in the interview. Some of this information will be garnered from the résumé in terms of education, experience, licenses, and certifications.

Motivation

You'll need to discover what motivates the candidates and then determine whether your unit and organization provide those types of motivators. Nurses need to be intrinsically motivated toward their jobs, meaning that they enjoy working toward meaningful goals, and they are motivated by learning and using their skills so that they stay challenged. Other intrinsic motivators include personal growth, helping others grow, and making a difference in someone else's life. Extrinsic motivators include money, recognition, status, power, title, and social status. You will be able to determine motivation during the interview by asking questions about what candidates liked best and least in their previous jobs. You will be able to tell from their responses if the current position is a good fit for them.

Opportunity

They will have plenty of opportunity to use most of their nursing skills, but will they have the opportunity to use all of their skills on your unit? You might be interviewing someone who loves to make presentations. Will he or she have the opportunity to do that while working on your unit? Although this isn't typically inherent in staff nurse roles, you might be able to find opportunities for him or her to use this skill. Someone else might love technology and although there is certainly some interaction with technology, will it be enough or might there be projects, such as an electronic health record rollout, where his or her talents could be used?

Culture

Will this person thrive in your organization's culture? You need to assess whether this would be a good fit for him or her. Therefore, it is important that you know what your cultural characteristics are. Find out what the candidate liked most and least about his or her previous organizations and determine how well these characteristics match your organization's. Some factors you will listen for include pace of change, recognition programs, opportunities for growth, opportunities for advancement, degree of autonomy, shared governance, etc. Determine whether the person's needs match what your organization offers.

Hiring the person who has the skills, motivation, and opportunity to use their skills, and who fits into your culture, means that person will be productive more quickly, enjoy more job satisfaction, and will tend to stay with you during good times and bad. This person will fit into your team better and enjoy collegial relationships if he or she is a good match for the job, you, your team, and the organization.

The Hiring Process

Hiring and interviewing practices at healthcare institutions vary. Most have a nurse recruiter who works in human resources who is responsible for screening résumés to check whether candidates have minimum qualifications (experience, education, licensing, certifications, etc.) and have passed any required testing. They often do phone interviews to begin the process of determining who needs to fall out of the process and who should move on to the next step. The focus in this chapter is on the interview process once a prequalified candidate comes to you. The process described is the same whether you are interviewing for a staff nurse position or an executive position.

The interview is a tool for finding the right person. The interviewing process is both a science and an art. Think of it as a qualitative research project. The science comes from using a solid process with each candidate (that will be described in this chapter). The art comes from your skill as an interviewer to glean the best information from the interviewees in the least amount of time. Not that you want to rush the process, but you want to stay away from asking questions that are irrelevant (which will waste your time and theirs) and potentially illegal. Considerations and suggestions on how to be an astute interviewer will also be described in this chapter.

Your goal is to find the person who has the knowledge, skills, and ability to meet the requirements of the job and who will fit into your organization. You want someone who will match your culture (values, mission, and vision) and be open to coaching and feedback—someone who wants to grow and reach his or her potential.

Elements of a sound interviewing process include:

- **Structure.** A structured interview process means that you will be asking the same questions to each candidate so that you can accurately compare the data among candidates. If you were to ask different questions of each person, it would be difficult, if not impossible, to make accurate comparisons among candidates.

- **Behavioral competencies.** Your questions should be focused on the behaviors that yield successful performance. You should have a list of competencies for the job and the questions you ask should be focused on these competencies. For example, if you were hiring an assistant nurse manager, some competencies might include:
    - Planning and organizing
    - Delegating
    - Coaching
    - Communicating
    - Team building
    - Collaborative decision-making

(See Calhoun et al. 2008 for a full list of competencies for healthcare leadership.) The goal is to determine what the candidate has done in the past to demonstrate skill in each area, with the premise being that past behavior predicts future behavior. Questions should be focused on what candidates have actually done in a particular situation and not on what they would do in a theoretical, future-oriented situation. Candidates should be able to answer your questions with an account of how they demonstrated that competency in the past. Try to get two examples for each competency. Determine whether the interviewees' responses are effective for the job in question or not.

- **Multiple interviewers.** You should not be the only person to interview the candidate. He or she should be interviewed by others, such as the recruiter, your colleagues (peers), your staff (potential peers of the candidate), and possibly your manager. Think of Olympic athletes. As they perform, they are observed and evaluated by a set of judges who are highly skilled at judging that sport. Each judge is observing the same performance, at the same time, with the same set of guidelines, from the same vantage point. Yet, we are often surprised how different the scores can be. So too during the interviewing process, getting different perspectives will enhance the quality of your decision and gain buy-in. Each of the interviewers should also have a structured, behavioral interview guide that will contain the questions they will ask. They will interview the candidate using some of the same competencies you use, but with different questions. The goal is for all competencies to be covered among the different interviews.

- **Assimilation.** All of the interviewers should have a conversation after all the interviews have been completed to review the results. If all the interviewers can't meet at the same time, the hiring manager—you—should at the least have a conversation with each of the other interviewers individually. It is optimal to get all interviewers together to review their observations on each competency and determine whether the candidate was able to demonstrate effective behavior for each.

Since it is important to find out at this point whether candidates are receptive to coaching, be sure to include questions about how they have been coached in the past. Finding out whether people are open to coaching and whether they really have accepted it and changed their behavior is critical. People who want to do a great job will be happy to get coaching so that they can be better at what they do. Be sure to get at least a few examples during the interview (see following examples).

Interviewing a staff nurse

When interviewing to fill a staff nurse position and wanting to determine whether candidates are open to coaching, you can ask a question such as:

- "Tell me about a time when you got some feedback and coaching from your charge nurse or nurse manager. What was the situation, what did you do, and what was the result of the interaction?"

Try to find an example of when candidates were coached for a positive behavior (reinforcement) and for an ineffective behavior (improvement). Be patient and give them some time to think of an example. If they can't think of an example on their own, you might prompt them with some examples:

- A communication (verbal or nonverbal) with a patient or colleague

- How they performed a technical procedure

- How they complied (or didn't comply) with a policy, etc.

Be sure their answers include:

- An account of the situation

- What they did

- The result

SCENARIO 1

Example from a Staff Nurse
A good example might sound like this:

"I remember this one time, I was working from 3 p.m. to 11 p.m. and the unit was really swamped. At around 8:00 p.m. the charge nurse asked me if I had taken my dinner break. I had been so busy for the entire shift I hadn't even thought about how hungry I was. I was really exhausted and had so many postops to check on. When she asked me to go on break, I sort of snapped at her and made a sarcastic crack like 'Yeah, right. I have time to eat.' She didn't appreciate my tone and said, very nicely, 'Linda, I didn't realize you were so busy but your tone of voice is a bit sharp. In the future, it would be helpful if you would come to me and let me know that you need help.' I felt badly that I snapped at her and apologized. It helped me realize that my tone can be prickly when I'm feeling overwhelmed so I actually appreciated her comment and the next time that situation happened, I went to her and told her so that she could get someone to help me."

If they don't describe all three parts, probe with follow-up questions. In this example, there is a situation, an action, and a result. Next, ask the candidate about another example. Try to get at least two examples for each competency or situation.

Interviewing a nurse leader

If you want to determine how nurse leader candidates approach coaching, ask a question like:

- "Tell me about a time when you needed to coach someone about an ineffective behavior. What was going on, what did you do, and what was the result?"

Lead! Becoming an Effective Coach and Mentor to Your Nursing Staff

---

SCENARIO 2

Example from a Nurse Leader
A good example might sound like this:

"In Labor and Delivery, our patient volume can become very heavy very quickly, and frequently I need to take care of patients so that my staff can get breaks. I was relieving a new nurse whose patient had an epidural. Since patients with epidurals can't feel their bladders, we have to keep a close eye on them. As I was doing an assessment of this patient, I noticed that her bladder was very full and I cathed her for one liter! When the nurse returned I had to coach her on the importance of being very vigilant of I&Os on patients who've had epidurals and to physically assess bladders frequently. She felt badly that she had overlooked this and appreciated the reminder. I've covered her patients since then and this situation has never happened again."

Here again, you can see the situation, the action, and the result. Ineffective coaching would have been if the manager had chastised the staff nurse or if the manager never said anything and put a note in her file for discussion during her performance review.

The Art of Interviewing

The first thing you want to do is to express appreciation for the candidate's interest in the position and in your organization. Since candidates may be nervous, it's best to begin the interview talking about the position, the organization, and yourself (your background and how you came to your position). This will help candidates relax and will demonstrate your interest in them. At this point, you also want to let them know the structure of the interview: the areas that will be discussed, how much time you plan to spend, that you will be taking notes, when they can ask you questions, and what the next steps will be once the interview is complete. This will also demonstrate to candidates that you are prepared, which will impress them. Be sure no one interrupts you during the interview; this demonstrates respect.

After welcoming candidates and giving them an overview of the interview process, ask them to walk you through their résumé, telling them that you read it, but want to discuss their background with them. This gets them talking about their previous jobs and education, which should be easy for them prior to the behavioral questions that can be more challenging, depending on how well they've prepared. As they go through each job they've held, ask them what they liked best, what they liked least, and why they left. This information will help you get at their motivation.

As you move to the behavioral questions, let candidates know the structure of the questions and how they should structure their answers. For example, you might say, "Now I'm going to ask you several questions about competencies that are necessary for this job. I'll be looking for what you have done in the past to demonstrate this skill. It would be very helpful if you could describe for me the situation or problem, what you did, and the outcome of your action." You should plan to spend around 10 minutes per competency and cover about seven or eight of the most important competencies during your interview.

After completing the behavioral questions, you'll need a minute to look back over your notes to see whether there is anything you missed. While you are reviewing your notes tell candidates to think about anything else they want to tell you about. Then give them the opportunity to do so. There may be an achievement or a project they want you to know about that did not come up during the interview.

Be sure to ask them what questions they have for you. Good candidates will have some questions prepared about the job, the organization, and you. They are also interviewing you to be sure that this role and organization are a good fit for them.

Explain your expectations

This is also the time to share your expectations with candidates. You should have a list of explicit expectations of how members of your unit work and interact with each other and patients.

Candidates need to hear your expectations to help determine whether this will be a good fit for them. If they have no idea how you expect them to perform and behave, they may have difficulty deciding whether to accept the position. We will further discuss setting expectations in the next chapter.

Close the interview with clear next steps

Close the interview with appreciation for candidates' time and interest and be very clear about what will happen next. It might include the next interview, drug testing, reference/background check, and/or when and how they will hear from you with your decision. You should get a thank-you note or e-mail from them within a day or two in which they will express appreciation for your consideration and their reaffirmed interest in the position.

Interviewing and hiring, like any other skill, take practice (see Figure 4.1 for some interview best practices). It is an art and like all artists, the more you do it, the better you get. You may want to do an occasional interview even if you don't have an immediate opening. You might sit in with others who are skilled and observe them as they interview. If you are looking for practice, ask your recruiter or colleagues if you can do some interviews with them. Get some coaching from someone who is skilled and can observe you during an interview and give you feedback. It takes practice to get a good rhythm going during interviews and to be able to elicit good behavioral information, so seek out those practice opportunities. Whom you hire is the most important decision you make. If you are not good at this, put it on your development plan and work with your manager and HR department to elevate your skills.

Last, it is very important that you leave candidates with a positive feeling about you, your organization, and themselves. At this point, this interview may be the only interaction they have had (other than with the nurse recruiter) with your hospital. You become the hospital. Whether they get the job or not, you want candidates to leave the interview with a good impression. Remember that candidates are self-selecting for your hospital and you. They can select out at any time. It is likely that they will tell other people about their interaction with you, and you want the "word on the street" about your hospital and you to be positive.

FIGURE 4.1 ■ INTERVIEWING BEST PRACTICES

Here are some things to remember during interviews:

- Maintain positive body language: smile, have a relaxed but interested posture, etc. Candidates will be able to think better if they stay relaxed.

- Take notes: Jot down key words that will help you remember their answers.

- Let candidates know the next step: when they will hear from you and how. Be specific with dates and mode of communication.

- Do not ask personal information. Any chitchat at the beginning of the interview can revolve around the weather, your directions, etc., but avoid personal questions (about kids, marital status, etc.). Your HR department has a list of illegal questions; if you keep your questions focused on the job, you will be safe.

- Watch your time; you are in control of the interview. If candidates start getting too verbose, gently redirect them as needed. Sit in view of a clock so that you can notice the time without having to look at your watch.

- Give candidates some positive feedback during the interview.

- If there will be another person sitting in on the interview, be sure to tell candidates ahead of time.

References

1. Calhoun, J. G., Dollett, L., Sinioris, M. E., Wainio, J. A., Butler, P. W., Griffith, J. R., & Warden, G. L. (2008) "Development of an interprofessional competency model for healthcare leadership." *Journal of Healthcare Management*, 53(6), 375–390.

2. Garman, A. N., & Johnson, M. P. (2006). "Leadership competencies: An introduction." *Journal of Healthcare Management*, 51(1), 13–17.

3. Hagevik, S. (2000). "Behavioral interviewing: Write a story, tell a story." *Journal of Environmental Health*, 62(7), 61.

SETTING GOALS AND EXPECTATIONS

Learning Objectives

After reading this chapter, the reader will be able to:

- Describe the difference between goals and expectations

- List some examples of expectations that should be explicit to your staff

You set the stage for trust and openness with your staff by setting clear goals and expectations, communicating them in a way that is understandable, and by gaining your staff's agreement on them. As a leader, you have a set of expectations in your mind for your staff. If these expectations are not clearly stated to your staff, staff will likely behave in a way that is in alignment with *their* set of expectations, which are based on *their* experience. Implicit expectations and ambiguous goals are dangerous to any relationship. When people are unaware of goals or are operating under a different set of expectations, simple misunderstandings or communication gaffes can turn into emotional flare-ups that can be severely damaging to the relationship.

Delineating explicit expectations is one way to build trust in a relationship. Communicating your expectations during the interview process, and again as the person joins your team, and then periodically to remind everyone helps reduce misunderstandings. Communicate goals and expectations verbally and in writing.

Determining Your Goals and Expectations

Goals and expectations are different. Goals are targets you strive for, and they should be challenging since the goals you have to stretch for motivate people to do their best and put forth effort. There is usually a metric tied to a goal. For example, you might have a goal to weigh 125 lb. That is a clear target. You know when you have achieved it. A fuzzy target would be "to lose weight." This is more of a wish, which may or may not affect your behavior.

Expectations, on the other hand, are descriptors of the manner in which a goal is achieved. Think of the goal as the *what* and an expectation as the *how* or the *norm of behavior.*

Goals

The goals you pick for your staff should be aligned with the goals of the hospital, which then cascade down to the units. Ideally, goals have a metric assigned to them. When determining a list of goals, use the SMART guide: *Specific, Measurable, Achievable, Relevant, Time-bound.*

Naturally, the goals will vary depending on level of leadership. Some examples of goal areas follow. All of the following are specific, measurable, achievable (depending on the metric and audience), and relevant (depending on the audience), and they will be time-bound as soon as you assign a date:

- Patient satisfaction

- Employee satisfaction

- Patient/visitor complaint rate

- Achievement rate of chargeable medications and supplies

- Incident report rates

- Number of training hours per staff member

- Promotion rate

- Use of agency nurses

- Committee participation

- Expense reduction

- Completion of a patient identification checklist prior to treatment or surgery

Here's an example of a SMART goal: "Each member of this unit will participate in 20 hours of training (clinical, communication, or leadership) prior to 12/31 of this year."

Examples of setting goals

A great example of how goal setting works is described in a paper by Baptist Health Care executives (Vermillion, Terry, Davis & Owens, 2010). The executive team set goals for the hospital under each of the hospital's five pillars: people, service, quality, financial performance, and growth. From there, the goals cascaded down throughout the organization to the unit or department level. Here are examples of the financial goals:

- Chief nursing officer (CNO): achieve operating margin* of 2%

- Service director: decrease RN agency use by 50% from the previous year

- Med-Surg manager: limit overtime to less than 2%

*Operating margin measures the proportion of an organization's revenue that is left over after paying for variable costs (expenses that vary based on patient census) of running the hospital, such as supplies, food, pharmaceuticals, water, etc. It is a measure of the financial health of the organization.

Here are examples of service goals:

- CNO: increase patient satisfaction to the 96th percentile

- Service director: increase patient satisfaction to the 97th percentile

- Cardiac pediatric manager: increase patient satisfaction to the 98th percentile

Here are examples of quality goals:

- CNO: decrease ventilator-related pneumonia by 3%

- Service director: decrease ventilator-related pneumonia by 3%

- Surgical ICU (SICU) manager: decrease ventilator-related pneumonia by 3%

Here are examples of people goals:

- CNO: decrease RN turnover to 10%

- Service director: decrease RN turnover to 8%

- Labor and delivery: decrease RN turnover to 7%

In the service examples, notice that not everyone has the same goal of getting to the 96th percentile that the CNO has. Goal determination must be equitable if everyone is going to buy-in and agree to the goal. As you know, certain areas inherently have higher patient satisfaction scores than others. Therefore, if a unit is starting with a patient satisfaction score of 85%, there wouldn't be much enthusiasm to ask them to achieve a jump to 96% in one year. Remember the "A" in SMART: achievable. Likewise, it would not be equitable to set a goal of 96% for a unit that already has a patient satisfaction score of 96%. To get everybody agreeing to the goals, the goals must be achievable and equitable.

Goal-setting theory affirms that in order to drive humans to put forth efforts, goals must be:

- Clear

- Challenging

- Agreed upon (Lycette & Herniman, 2008)

Goals that are *clear* should have a metric and a date assigned to them; if that is not the case, the goal should be behavioral and leave no room for ambiguity. Examples of behavioral goals (both with and without metrics attached) follow:

- **Clear goal:** develop and promote at least one nurse before 12/31 of this year

- **Ambiguous goal:** develop your staff for leadership positions

The clear goal leaves no room to wonder what you need to shoot for. It gives you a target to shoot for and will likely motivate you to get to work thinking about how you are going to achieve the goal. It will cause a behavior change in you that is focused, versus the ambiguous "goal" of developing your staff, which might lead you to some actions that are diffuse (all staff attend a leadership workshop) or none at all.

Not all goals include metrics. You might have a goal to complete your Master of Nursing degree by January 1 of next year. Although there is no metric, you will certainly know when you have met your goal since this statement meets all the other criteria for a SMART goal. It is specific; your diploma will be your measurement; and it is achievable (assuming you have your Bachelor of Science and course work toward your Master of Science [MS] started, etc.), relevant, and time-bound.

A good goal is *challenging*. Think back to Chapter 1 and the discussion about "flow." You are typically performing at your best when the task is not easy, but is challenging. Remember also that the highest motivator is self-actualization. Therefore, challenging goals that are relevant and realistic will motivate your behavior more than will easy goals. However, the reverse is also true: A goal that is too difficult to achieve will demotivate you. A goal needs to be both challenging and attainable in order to bring out the best efforts in your group (Livingston, 2003).

- **Challenging goal:** reduce falls by 10%

- **Easy goal:** reduce falls by 1%

Which one of the goals listed earlier is more likely to change your behavior and lead to better results? Of course, the more ambitious goal. "High goals and expectations lead to high performance" (Kouzes & Posner, 2002). Achievement of challenging goals should be accompanied by support, feedback, rewards, and recognition to encourage continuance of achievement (Lycette & Herniman, 2008). Interestingly, leaders who have high expectations of themselves tend to have higher expectations of their employees. It seems that there is a subtle transference of their self-image to their employees yielding higher results for both manager and direct report (Livingston, 2003).

People need to accept the goal and *agree* to work toward it in order for it to be motivating. As with decision-making in a shared governance model, input into the goal-setting process helps increase acceptance of the goal. It helps give staff some control in goal determination and hence, more buy-in into it. Cunningham and Austin (2007) describe their study to improve safety in operating rooms by increasing the practice of hands-free technique for the transfer of sharp surgical instruments. They used participative goal setting with the staff so that they, the staff, could establish an achievable and realistic goal. The inpatient operating room (OR) staff started with 32% compliance with the hands-free policy. They set a goal of 45% compliance, and achieved a result of 64% compliance. The outpatient OR staff started with a similar 31% compliance rate, set a goal of 75% compliance, and achieved the result of 70%. The point is that both teams realized remarkable success, which can be at least partially attributed to the fact that the staff set the goal for this study.

Next time you want to improve a metric, get input from your staff on what they feel is a reasonable and achievable goal. Get their ideas on how to make it happen. Moreover, always give positive feedback and recognition for success along the way.

Objectives to accomplish a goal

The steps you need to take to accomplish a goal are the objectives. It is helpful to write deadline dates next to each objective (see Figure 5.1). So, if you have a goal to complete your MS by a certain date, some of the objectives to reach that goal might include:

- Investigate colleges that offer the program that you are interested in: February

- Find out what is involved in the application process: March

- Take the GREs: April

- Get references: May

- Have transcripts sent: May

- Determine your start date and the curriculum: June

FIGURE 5.1 ■ SETTING GOALS

Think about a professional goal you have. Does it fit the criteria for a SMART goal? Write out your goal and the objectives to complete it.

Goal

Specific: _____

Measurable: _____

Achievable: _____

Relevant: _____

Time-bound: _____

Objectives

Determine the objectives that must be met to achieve your goal:

_____

_____

_____

After you have thought about your own goals, think about a goal for each of your staff or for your unit.

EXAMPLE

Unit Goals

A goal for your unit could be to reduce falls by 10% this year. The objective would be to round every hour on each patient.

Another goal might be to reduce incidents of catheter-associated urinary tract infections (CAUTI) by x%. An objective would be to implement the CAUTI prevention plan with each patient who has a catheter.

Expectations

Everybody brings expectations to almost every situation. When starting a new job, new employees have an expectation of what the job will be like and how they will be treated. When expectations don't match reality, people get hurt, communication fails, and productivity decreases. Too often, good, well-intentioned employees leave. There needs to be an explicit exchange of expectations; the job interview is a great time to communicate to the candidate exactly what your expectations are. This way there are no surprises. It is also a good practice to ask candidates what their expectations are of you, the job, the team, and the organization. However, this is rarely done and disenfranchisement ensues. Unfortunately, the absence of this practice wastes time, money, and immense emotional energy.

So often, you might not even be aware of what your expectations are without some reflection. A good practice for managers is to write down your expectations and periodically review and update the list (see Figure 5.2). Your expectations are a reflection of the organizational culture, the subculture that you have developed in your department, and your own past experiences. Since the culture is "the way we do things around here," your expectations are likely to be second nature to you. However, new-comers won't know what these behaviors are and may make several mistakes and assumptions based on their own experiences. It is a good practice to make these known up front and then role model the behaviors you expect from others.

FIGURE 5.2 ■ SETTING EXPECTATIONS

Since expectations are the norm of behavior or the "how we do things around here," consider which areas would be helpful to explicitly express to new staff, and which areas you can remind experienced staff about. Consider the following:

- **How we treat each other**
  - Respect
  - Trust
  - Manners
- **Meetings**
  - Who attends which meetings
  - Who facilitates meetings
  - Are people expected to express ideas?
  - Is conflict allowed?
  - Are start and end times adhered to?
  - Are staff allowed to attend meetings during regular shift time? If not, is overtime pay allowed?
- **Communication**
  - Who communicates with whom
  - Can staff members talk to the director instead of talking to you (the manager) first?
  - How are disagreements worked out: between staff, physicians, other colleagues?
- **Project work**
- **Must project work be completed on time? What if that becomes impossible?**
- **How often do you need to be updated on project status?**
- **Shift coverage/calling in late/illness**
- **What types of events do you expect to be notified about?**
  - During the daytime
  - At night
- **How does one get promoted into a leadership position?**
- **Coaching**
  - Is it expected that staff can coach each other and be open to coaching?

As you can see in Figure 5.2, many of these situations are typically not written down anywhere. Writing them down and communicating them with your staff will help avoid much turmoil and wasted time. It's also a good idea to get staff's ideas about other topics. Otherwise, people will operate under the assumption that they should handle issues here the same way they've handled them in other places in the past.

LEADERSHIP TIP

Here is a simple example of how some basic expectations can be communicated to your staff.

One of your expectations of your assistant nurse managers might be: "Project work will be completed by the date that we all agreed to. If it cannot be completed by the agreed-on date due to an emergency, you should let me know immediately by phone or e-mail. Do not just show up with uncompleted work since this will put all of us behind on our combined project obligations."

Ask whether there are any questions about this expectation and whether they can agree to comply. This expectation should also be put in writing (along with your other expectations).

An expectation of your staff might be that any inappropriate behavior by other staff or colleagues be addressed by the nurse and the other party (assuming they have the necessary skills to have this kind of a discussion. If they don't, you need to give them some training on confrontations.) You might say that you are willing and happy to offer coaching and support on how to conduct this discussion, but that you will not be the mediator of conflict that hasn't been addressed first by the two parties. Staff should come to you to intervene in the situation only after a resolution has been tried by the parties first.

Ensure understanding of this expectation by asking staff to tell you what they understand to have heard or asking whether they have any questions. Ask whether they can agree to do this.

Al Stubblefield (2005) describes expectations as "standards of performance" at Baptist Health Care. The extensive list of standards is shown to all candidates during their interviews to be sure they understand that the standards are indeed part of the culture and they will be held accountable to them. This gives candidates a realistic preview of what it is like to work at Baptist and it gives them the opportunity to deselect themselves from the process if they choose. Included on the Baptist list of "standards of performance" are specific descriptions for behavior in each of these areas: "attitude, appearance, communication, call lights, commitment to coworkers, customer waiting, elevator etiquette, privacy, safety awareness, sense of ownership" (Stubblefield, 2005). This is a great example of how to impart and embed the culture.

Having SMART goals and objectives and explicit expectations is helpful to everyone. Time isn't wasted guessing how one should behave to get along with peers and with you. Take the time to be sure your goals and objectives are as measurable or as observable as possible. Be sure they challenge your staff to stretch out of their comfort zones so that they grow and stay engaged. Write down your expectations and communicate them to the staff. This might be a good exercise to do with your leadership team and staff so that there is input and agreement from them. The benefits will be well worth the effort.

References

1. Cunningham, T. R., & Austin, J. (2007). "Using goal setting, task clarification, and feedback to increase the use of the hands-free technique by hospital operating room staff." *Journal of Applied Behavior Analysis*, 40(4), 673–766.

2. Kouzes, J. M., & Posner, B. Z. (2002). *The Leadership Challenge* (3rd ed.). San Francisco: Jossey-Bass.

3. Livingston, J. S. (2003). "Pygmalion in management. *Harvard Business Review*, 81(1), 97–106.

4. Lycette, B., & Herniman, J. (2008). "New goal-setting theory." *Industrial Management*, 50(5). 25–31.

5. Stubblefield, A. (2005). *The Baptist Health Care Journey to Excellence*. Hoboken, NJ: John Wiley & Sons, Inc.

6. Vermillion, K., Terry, A., Davis, S., & Owens, K. (2010). "Innovations in performance management." *Healthcare Financial Management*, 64(5), 98–104.

CHAPTER 6

COACHING & MENTORING INTERPERSONAL COMMUNICATION

Learning Objectives

After reading this chapter, the reader will be able to:

- Describe why nonverbal communication is so important

- Explain the steps of the listening process

"What you do speaks so loud that I cannot hear what you say."
—Ralph Waldo Emerson

Communication is a foundational competency for any leader. It is one of the most important ways that relationships and trust are built. It is how we connect with others as human beings and relay what is important to us and how we understand what is important to them. Since everyone has different hardwiring and different experiences and different lenses, it is obvious why so much miscommunication occurs.

We each see and experience life in a unique way and our interpretations of the behaviors of the next person may be different from someone else's. We observe, interpret meaning, and draw conclusions that may be completely inaccurate (Stone, Patton & Heen, 1999). Open and honest exchange of information with each other helps to ensure that we have the correct and complete picture. In a healthcare setting, where a mistake can have lethal consequences, communication prevents errors.

Communication is often viewed as a soft skill—one that is touchy feely. Many people recoil from the topic and avoid training on this skill. They feel their technical skills or "smarts" mean they are above it. However, no amount of cognitive ability can make up for poor interpersonal communications. This becomes even more apparent as emotions build in a relationship or conversation. As emotions intensify, IQ seems to diminish. Daniel Goleman (1995) refers to this as an emotional hijacking. We say and do things we regret, or that at least do not have the desired effect.

The soft skill is, in reality, a hard skill. Many of the thorny problems that most managers have to wrestle with can be traced back to poor communications skills. Every day you have to interact with your direct reports, colleagues, peers, and your manager. Every day you have to attend to what you say, and more importantly, how you say it. But, what would happen to your relationships if you decided to listen before speaking?

Avoiding Communication Problems

There is parable of six blind men who were asked, "What is an elephant?" Each of the men were presented with one part of an elephant: foot, back, tail, tusk, trunk, ears. Not surprisingly, each man had a different assessment of what an elephant was, depending on the part that he touched. True to human nature, each one was 100% sure that their assessment was correct and proceeded to argue with one another about what this "elephant" was like.

How often have we been in the position of holding stubbornly to our opinions of situations because we are so confident that our assessments are correct? Here's the rub: We may have a perfectly logical assessment of a situation and may even be correct; we just don't always have the complete picture. And, if we are right, that doesn't necessarily mean others must be wrong. It is natural to arrive at conclusions based on the information we have. But it is critical to remember that most likely we don't have *all* the information. There are many circumstances in which we have to make a decision and act without having all the information. In fact, this is often the norm. The world changes so quickly and information comes at us so quickly and continuously, we can't wait until we have it all. If we did, we would never act.

However, it behooves us to ask others for their input since it is guaranteed that their perspectives differ from our own, even if slightly. What usually happens when perspectives are different (like with the six blind men) is that we dig into the correctness of our own view and our own reality and then commence proving it to others. When that happens, emotions rise and the brain knots up, unable to reason and think clearly; you start to figuratively "go blind" (Patterson et al., 2002). The stress response is activated and either an argument ensues or one or both parties flee or at least shut down. Communication is over.

Wouldn't it make more sense if the six blind men talked to each other in an attempt to assemble the correct picture? If they had put their information *together*, they would have been much more likely to create an accurate picture of an elephant. Experience has shown that in the majority of instances, group decisions are better than individual decisions. They take more time, but they are usually more precise. Why then don't we listen more to others' opinions and observations? Because we assume that if we are right, then others must be wrong. This sets up an adversarial relationship that ignites the stress response.

Hence, there is a really good case for listening, even if you are 100% sure that the "tail" is a rope; a tail is certainly not a rope and a rope is surely not an elephant.

The case for listening

As a manager, make listening a priority and practice (read: role model) it in front of your staff and colleagues. Remember, you are always role modeling to others, whether you realize it or not. People pay much more attention to what you do than to what you say. So, be the message. Be the change agent.

L E A D E R S H I P   T I P

Listening is one of the best ways to show respect for someone.

Behaviors and attitudes to show you are an avid listener:

1. **Clear your mind.** Set your opinions aside so that you can *really* listen to what the other person is saying and not think about the similarities to or differences from what you think. Clear your mind so that you are not formulating your reply. Pretend that you have not touched the elephant. Be open to hearing about the "wall" that the speaker touched without comparing it to the "rope" that you touched. Appreciate that, as opposed to the person being crazy, he or she holds a perspective that may be very different from yours. Try not to reconcile these perspectives while the other person is talking or you will miss some valuable information that you need to complete the picture.

2. **Listen for feelings.** Listening for feelings should preempt listening for content. As someone is talking to you, pay attention to the feelings that are behind the content. This will help you to correctly diagnose the real problem, which has to happen before a solution can be rendered.

    Everyone has experienced being upset with someone, but when that person asked you what was wrong, you said, "Nothing." Too frequently people take this at face value, listen only for content, and don't pay attention to the feeling behind it. Had the person felt the feeling you were feeling and said something like, "I can see that you are upset and I'd really like to know what happened," he or she would have acknowledged your anger and opened the door to gaining the information he or she needed to hear—the content. This acknowledgment validates you. Everyone wants to feel validated but too often, well-intentioned people don't take the extra step. Seeing a situation from the perspective of another helps the communication process.

It can be intimidating to make a statement about what another is feeling; it makes us vulnerable. We might be wrong. However, it is critical in order for true communication to take place.

"The most important thing in communication is hearing what isn't said."
—Peter F. Drucker

How do you listen for feelings? Basically, you need to listen with your heart, eyes, and ears (Covey, 1989). You need to pay attention to the nonverbals that are being communicated. To notice incongruence between verbal and nonverbal communication, you must pay attention to it. Listen for the whole message. Notice the person's tone of voice, their pace, volume, and inflections. If their nonverbals are not congruent with what they are saying, ask a question or make a statement to open the door to let them say what they are truly feeling. Also notice their posture, gestures, eye contact, and facial expressions. If something doesn't feel right to you, give them the opportunity express what is truly on their mind. Your ability and comfort with exploring what is going on with them will not only help you get the entire picture, but will help build trust with them as well.

It is best to practice these skills in a safe environment prior to using them when emotions might be running high or when you are caught off guard. Become an observer of human behavior and notice when verbal communication and non-verbal communication are out of sync and when they are aligned. That way, when an unanticipated situation arises when you need to employ this skill, you will be ready.

3. **Listen for content.** If you have correctly listened for feelings, listening for content will be much easier. Not everybody communicates his or her thoughts in a logical manner, so you will still need to be sure that you are hearing the correct message.

4. **Explore.** Check for understanding by reiterating what you understood the person to say and mean. This should not sound canned, as if you are parroting back exactly what was said, but should be stated in a way that makes sense to you. It is surprising how often you might think you understand exactly what was said and intended only to find out that you are wrong. So restate what you heard to be certain you are correct. If you don't have a clear picture of the situation and need more information, ask exploring questions. These questions should usually be open-ended and might sound like this:

   - Tell me what led up to the conversation.
   - What was her demeanor like?
   - How did you choose the timing of the conversation?
   - What other options did you review with him?
   - When you laughed, what was his reaction?

5. **Express appreciation.** Always thank someone for opening up to you and sharing his or her thoughts and feelings. You should also express appreciation for sharing your thoughts and feelings with someone else. Taking the time to listen to the whole message validates us as humans. In this high-tech world of texts and tweets, these types of real conversations seem to be becoming less frequent. But they are necessary for our human development, personal satisfaction in our social groups, and our self-esteem.

Just as physicians know that listening to their patients is important in order to provide the best possible care *and* to decrease malpractice risk, nurse leaders should listen to their staff to be the best possible coach and mentor to them and to decrease "flight risk." Whether members of your staff come to you with ideas or with suggestions for change, honor them by really listening to what they are taking the time to share with you. Showing them respect will aid in keeping them with you and engaged in what they are doing.

The case for paying attention to your nonverbal communication

Typically, when the word *communication* is brought up, thoughts tend to center on the spoken word only. People spend a lot of time thinking about what they are going to say. That's a good thing, especially when emotions are running high and speaking off the cuff becomes dangerous. However, most of the meaning of your communication comes not from what you say, but how you say it. In fact, research has suggested that 93% of our communication is nonverbal. When crafting a communication, who spends 93% of their time crafting their nonverbals? We should! You should devote time to planning your nonverbal communication, especially when the interaction is really important.

When you are planning a serious conversation, of course you are going to think about what you say. But, you should put even more effort into the way you say it by considering the desired effect of your two areas of nonverbals:

- **Voice:** volume, pace, tone, inflections

- **Visual:** posture, eye contact, gestures, facial expressions

Voice

Consider how your voice sounds depending on the communication you want to send. For example, if you have coached someone on a particular behavior that must change to avoid disciplinary action, and now need to confront him or her on it, your voice is an important part of the message. Your voice needs to be serious (tone). You need to avoid lots of inflections, and the pace and volume should be steady. Your voice must match the seriousness of the content.

Conversely, if you are coaching someone on a positive behavior, one that you want him or her to continue, your voice should have a lighter tone, one that is more congratulatory. During a confrontation or during praise, think about how your voice should sound.

People will always believe your nonverbal communication over your verbal communication.

CASE STUDY

Disciplinary Confrontation

During a confrontation, Sonia, a nurse manager, had to begin a disciplinary process with one of the technicians on the unit, Maria. Sonia asked one of her nurse leaders to sit in on the conversation for two reasons. She wanted to role model what the discussion should sound and look like and she also wanted an observer in the room. The meeting went well and Sonia maintained composure, both sounding and looking like the meeting was serious, which it was. The nurse leader, who had a very affiliative personality, felt a bit uncomfortable with the tone of the meeting. Just as Sonia was wrapping up the interaction, the nurse leader cracked a joke to change the mood in the room, which, of course, changed the tone and altered the impact of the confrontation.

Portraying Confidence

A nursing director, Isabella, who was new in her position, was feeling insecure about "knowing it all" and was having trouble communicating with authority to her colleagues. The chief nursing officer (CNO) noted that Isabella's voice was shaky and wavered. She spoke too quickly and her vocal pitch was too high. Her nervousness was conveyed to her colleagues. They could not get past the sound of her voice to believe that she knew what she was doing (which she did, although she didn't yet feel confident). The CNO gave Isabella feedback after each time that she spoke and coached her to practice in the mirror: to slow down her pace and lower her pitch and volume. After practicing her presentations and changing her self-talk, Isabella was able to communicate the information in a way that left her colleagues feeling that she was in control of the situation.

Visual

Your posture and eye contact are the two most important visual nonverbals that affect your communication. Standing up straight, on two feet with your weight evenly distributed (as opposed to listing to one side) communicates confidence and calmness. Slouching, or standing with weight on one side is not a leader-like stance. Take a look in the mirror; it makes a big difference. Incorporate the following visual nonverbals:

- Eye contact should be direct, but not piercing.

- Gestures should be used for emphasis, but should not be distracting. The more serious the content, the fewer the gestures.

- Facial expressions should be aligned with the verbal message.

Let's examine the scenarios listed previously. First, there is Sonia's confrontation. If you are sitting for this conversation, you should sit still without fidgeting or bouncing your foot. Sit up straight. Maintain steady eye contact and keep your gestures to a minimum. Do not smile while confronting someone or giving them a verbal warning. You want them to know this is serious business. If you are smiling and slouching and using lots of animated facial gestures, they will not think you are serious. How could they? So for these types of conversations, really think about how you want to look and sound so the person you're confronting really gets the message. Laughing and smiling lightens the intended gravitas of the communication.

In the other example, the nursing director, Isabella, felt nervous and insecure but wanted and needed to look authoritative. Her feelings of anxiety tended to make her want to slouch (get smaller) and fidget or shift weight back and forth. When giving her presentations, she needed to stand up straight and on two feet with weight evenly distributed. This is a powerful stance. She needed to maintain good eye contact and a pleasant facial expression. Smiling is usually fine except when the news is dire; however, too much smiling or laughing can connote nervousness.

Planning Nonverbal Communication

Whether you are planning a confrontation or some other difficult conversation, or a presentation where you think you will be uncomfortable and nervous, giving some thought to your feelings ahead of time will help you plan for and control them. Likewise, if you think ahead of time about what the other person(s) will be feeling, you can plan for their reactions. Forethought and planning helps prevent "emotional hijacking" (Goleman, 1995) on your part and theirs. Your message has a much better chance of being communicated and received as intended. See Figure 6.1 for a tool to help you plan.

FIGURE 6.1 ■ PRACTICING NONVERBAL COMMUNICATION

Next time you need to communicate and you feel that you might be anxious, plan the following:

- **What is the message I want to send? Plan your verbal communication:**
  - What you will say
  - How you will say it
- **How do I need to send the communication? How must I look and sound in order to be in sync with the content?**
- **How should my voice sound? Consider:**
  - Volume
  - Pace
  - Tone
  - Inflections
- **How should my visuals appear? Consider:**
  - Posture
  - Eye contact
  - Gestures
  - Facial expressions

Practice your nonverbal communication when your message is really important. That includes when sharing good news or bad news. If you are sharing good news, but never smile or use facial expressions or voice intonations, people may detect a misalignment and wonder whether you are telling the full truth. If you are happy, show it. If you're not happy, show it. Be sure that the 93% nonverbal portion of your communication is matched to the verbal content. Spend at least as much time giving thought to and planning the nonverbal as the verbal component of your message.

The following is an example where the manager didn't plan what he was going to say or how he was going to have a sensitive conversation with his assistant nurse manager, nor did he think about and plan for how the assistant nurse manager would feel.

CASE STUDY

Planning Avoids Missteps

Robert, a nurse manager, received a note from an unhappy patient who complained about the care she received from Beth, who Robert knows is a very good assistant nurse manager. The patient's comments about Beth were very harsh and not at all reflective of Beth's usual great care.

Robert had to share the note with Beth. He did not open the discussion with some positive comments about how atypical the patient's comments were and he did not plan for Beth's reaction, which was likely to be hurt feelings. Robert just gave her the note. There was no setting the stage and no empathy for Beth's likely reaction.

Needless to say, when Beth read the note, she started crying. She was just coming off the night shift and was very tired, and the note upset her greatly.

Robert gave no thought to the communication before it took place. He didn't plan his verbal or nonverbal communication to lessen the blow of the patient's comments. Had he given some foresight to this interaction, he might have been able to help preserve Beth's self-esteem and then had a discussion about what had actually happened with this particular patient interaction. Instead, he ended up with a hurt nurse who wasn't able to discuss what had actually happened.

As a manager, you are always communicating, whether or not you are speaking. You are always role modeling behavior and communication to others. People will always be interpreting what you say and do through their lenses. That is why you need to attend to your words and to your actions or lack thereof. Staff might assume that if you are not interacting with them, that everything is okay. Or they might assume that something bad is on the horizon. This might be true. If it is true, they need to know it. And if it isn't, it's time to send the correct message.

References

1. Covey, S. R. (1989). *The 7 Habits of Highly Effective People.* New York: Fireside.

2. Covey, S. R. (1990). *Principle-Centered Leadership.* New York: Summit Books.

3. Goleman, D. (1995). *Emotional Intelligence.* New York: Bantam Books.

4. Patterson, K., Grenny, J., McMillan, R., Switzler, A. (2002). *Crucial Conversations.* New York: McGraw-Hill.

5. Stone, D., Patton, B., & Heen, S. (1999). *Difficult Conversations.* New York: Penguin Books.

FEEDBACK

Learning Objectives

After reading this chapter, the reader will be able to:

- Define feedback
- List ways to gather feedback

Suppose you were taking a class where none of your tests, papers, or projects was ever returned to you. How would you know whether you needed to put more time into the course and study harder or whether you were getting the important concepts?

What about saving for retirement? Most of us have some money deducted from our paychecks every month that is automatically deposited into our retirement account. Are we saving enough? If we don't check at least annually and make projections forward, how will we know whether we have enough to retire at the desired age?

Without feedback, you have no idea whether you need to change your behavior so you can be more effective and meet your goals. You're operating in a vacuum and making assumptions that all is well. And all might be well, but you don't know. Not knowing is stressful and does not motivate you to put forth effort toward achieving goals.

Why Feedback Is Important

Nurses *want* your feedback. They want to know how they are doing and what they could do to be more effective. They want to know what they are doing well and the behaviors they should continue.

Feedback motivates you to either continue what you are doing or change your behavior to attain challenging goals, produce results, and enjoy the rewards and satisfaction of greater performance. Feedback gives a reference point, a mileage marker to provide you with the satisfaction of knowing how far you have come and what you need to do to reach the "finish line." Individuals and teams need to know where they stand relative to the goal (Lycette & Herniman, 2008.)

In a recent study, nurses said feedback from peers, management, physicians, and patients was important and resulted in overall job satisfaction and a sense of security about doing a good job (Christiansen, 2008). Nurses want to do a good job, but need to know when they are doing it and when they are not. Most nurses claim they don't get enough feedback.

Trust is built through the practice of giving and receiving honest, supportive feedback. Feedback is a form of open communication. Its absence connotes a closed communication environment, which may not be reality but that will likely be the takeaway perception.

Since the feedback process takes preparation, planning, and time, it also demonstrates that you care about the person. When you feel that your manager really cares about your success, and is patiently willing to help you achieve your goals, your intent to stay will likely increase.

To summarize, sharing feedback:

- Confirms competence

- Builds confidence in performing current tasks

- Builds confidence to take risks

- Leads to improved performance

- Builds trust

- Promotes job satisfaction

- Shows you care—builds relationships

- Is what nurses want

Deciding When to Provide Input

So you have decided that sharing feedback with your staff is a good idea. How do you determine which behaviors to give feedback on? A good place to start is the list of goals, objectives, clinical standards, and expectations. This list should include most of the behaviors that are necessary for excellence: both "what" and "how." Look at what your staff do, and the results they realize, and how they do it.

Data collection methods include direct observation, patient records, reviewing care plans, talking with patients, talking with coworkers, talking directly with the nurse (Carter, 1992), and doing a survey where you get anonymous input from coworkers and colleagues.

This may sound like a daunting task, and you may feel that you don't have time for all of it. Let's break it down into a manageable piece of work. If you have a very large staff, you will need assistance from your nurse leaders; they will need to be trained on this process.

Chapter 7

How to collect data

There are many ways you can go about this, but since you can't be with every staff nurse every day, all day, here are two ideas with possible time frames listed for each activity.

Option A

1. Select one nurse per week on whom you will collect data.

2. Spend some time working with her. Let her know what you are doing. Observe her with her patients, other staff, physicians, etc. You will be able to observe her clinical skills and determine whether she is meeting your expectations on how the job gets done. Even though the Hawthorne effect (people's behavior changes when they are being observed) might come into play here, you'll be surprised how much data you will be able to gather—both positive and developmental. Time: 2 hours

3. Talk to the nurse's patients and read her patient record information. Time: 15 minutes

4. Interview a few colleagues who regularly work with her (privately). Find out what they think are her strengths and what she should develop. Get examples. Remind them this all to help the nurse. Promise to keep their comments anonymous unless they don't mind being identified. Time: 30 minutes

5. Talk to a few physicians and other colleagues on the service with whom she interacts. Get examples of her strengths and developmental areas. Time: 30 minutes

6. Talk to your admin, technicians, and patient care associates (PCAs). Ask them the same questions and get examples of the nurse's strengths and developmental areas. Time: 15 minutes

7. Write up your report. Time: 1 hour

8. Have a feedback conversation with the staff nurse. Time: 1 hour

Total approximate time in data collection phase per nurse: five hours. You should schedule this activity for each staff nurse at least twice per year, which would take 10 hours per staff nurse. This is not a lot of time to devote to each nurse who touches your patients.

EXAMPLE

Here's an example from another industry to put this into perspective. In the pharmaceutical industry, it is universally agreed that the most important segment of the organization is the sales force since they are the ones who have direct interaction with the customers: the physicians and pharmacists. Therefore, it is standard practice that the district sales manager spends *four out of five days per week* with their sales consultants calling on doctors in their offices or hospital. It is typical that each sales representative spends about *8–10 days per year* working with their manager, who is giving them real-time feedback and coaching and support. District sales managers may spend 64–80 hours per year directly observing and coaching each sales consultant as they call on their customers vs. 10 hours per year suggested previously for each of your nurses.

Option B

Another way to collect data is to design a survey and e-mail it to all the respondents who you feel have observed the nurse in her work setting enough to give some feedback. This survey can be designed using job competencies, expectations, etc., with room for comments from the respondents. The human resources (HR) department can help you design this and it can be sent out using one of the online survey instruments (SurveyMonkey™, Zoomerang®, etc.).

You'll also need to do some observation and patient interviews to add to the survey results, but that should give you a wealth of data to share.

You may choose either of the two options discussed earlier or you may create one of your own that fits your unit better. Just be sure that the system you select is equitable for everyone, with the caveat that the most inexperienced nurses will probably need the most feedback.

Of course, in your regular interaction with staff and patients, you'll be able to collect data even when you aren't really looking for it. Just be sure to quickly document everything you see and hear that you want to share so that it doesn't slip your mind.

LEADERSHIP TIP

Remember, giving feedback is probably the most impactful skill development tool you have, and developing your staff to give great patient care is the most important component of your job.

How to Give Feedback

Feedback starts with goals, objectives, and expectations and is the first step in the coaching process. Feedback contains the following elements, which will describe behavior related to goals, objectives, and expectations:

- A description of the situation

- A description of what the person said or did

- A description of the *effect* it had on others (patients or staff) or on a process

Feedback does not include what the person could do differently—that's coaching. Feedback merely describes what happened and the effect. The next two chapters will cover coaching.

Feedback must be specific and timely

Good feedback needs to be *specific* as opposed to general in order to reinforce behavior or effect a change. For example, general "feedback" might be: "Good job helping with that emergency earlier." That type of comment is nice, but it doesn't include the elements of feedback that make it specific. Good feedback might sound like this: "Thanks for helping with that precipitous delivery earlier when three of the staff were already tied up with that stat C-section. You really did a great job calling the resident, helping Theresa by opening up the delivery kit, and then taking care of the baby after the delivery and talking to the dad. I could tell Theresa felt so much more confident and relaxed by being able to focus just on the delivery."

The example above has the following:

- A situation: The floor was very busy and short-handed

- An action: The nurse made the call, took care of the baby, and talked to the dad

- An effect: Theresa was more confident and relaxed and focused because the nurse was there handling other things

This type of feedback is likely to reinforce the nurse's behavior and cause her to repeat it in the future. It also shows that the nurse was meeting your expectations on how you treat colleagues: in a pleasant, helpful, supportive manner that is typical of a well-functioning team.

Feedback also needs to be *timely*. Feedback is most effective when it occurs as close to the event as possible. As time flies by, our memories fade and feedback loses its power. Think about the example earlier. If this feedback had been given to the OB nurse three weeks after the event or, even worse, months later at an appraisal discussion, it would have been meaningless and would not have had much motivating horsepower to reinforce the nurse's behavior. Always give feedback as close to the event as you can if you want to get the most charge out of it.

How to Communicate Feedback

1. Let everyone who may be involved in the process know what you are doing and why. Those who may be involved in the process on a typical nursing unit include:

- Your staff (nurses, patient care assistants, administrative assistants, technicians)

- Staff and management on other units in your service (colleagues)

- Your manager

- Physician colleagues

You already give feedback to your staff, but if you intend to give feedback a heightened focus with a subsequent change in your behavior (you'll be doing a lot of observing and asking questions), staff need to know the details of this new focus. They will need to receive a communication from you informing them about the purpose and the goal of giving them increased feedback. Your communication should include the following:

- The definition of feedback and why it is important (leads to improved job satisfaction, job performance, confidence, etc.).

- That your intention is to help your staff be more effective and reach their goals and the goals of the unit.

- Your actions: Describe what you will be doing, such as your methods for data gathering, that you will be asking them for feedback on other staff, what feedback conversations entail, etc.

- How they can help you: They should note (they already notice) what your staff do that is very effective and what they do that they could improve upon. Let them know you are looking for balanced feedback; that is, you want feedback on both positive behaviors and less-than-positive behaviors.

- An expression of appreciation and inviting questions.

Periodically send updates to this group to let them know how the program is going, express appreciation again, and let them know whether there is anything else they need to do to help you help your staff (more specifics, etc.).

2. Be sure the feedback you give is accurate: Check your accuracy. Do you have all the facts? Do they need to be checked, or do a few additional questions need to be asked? Are you operating with any assumptions? If so, check the validity.

3. Set the climate. State your intentions and be sure the receiver is open to some feedback (do not rush). Is he or she presently receptive to feedback? Staff need to be taught what feedback is and how to take an active role in the interaction. Bing-You, Bertsch, Thompson (1998) developed a formalized program at Maine Medical Center to increase medical students' receptivity to feedback (and coaching) by increasing their participation in the discussion and process. A training program was developed for the students to help them understand the process and take an active role in it. Some of the elements that the feedback recipients (the medical students) needed to take responsibility for included:

- Ensuring that the feedback discussion transpired in a quiet place without interruptions (feedback "on the fly" is generally not a good idea)

- Maintaining and updating a list of learning objectives that they were working on, and sharing that with the feedback provider

- Sharing a self-assessment of what he or she has accomplished in relation to the learning objectives

- Being open with areas of specific concern

- Giving feedback on the feedback

4. Open the feedback session by asking some open-ended questions. For example, "Tell me about what happened with ___." That will help you gain the person's perspective of the situation; it will disclose to you the lens through which he or she viewed the situation. Remember, if you are giving feedback based only on your observation (which is fine) and if you haven't checked out this situation with others, you have only your lens on. So ask for the person's assessment of the situation whether the feedback is positive or developmental. Remember to cover the three elements of feedback:

- Situations

- Actions

- The effect of the actions—ask feedback recipients what they see as the effect of their actions

5. Express appreciation and give encouragement. Encouragement is a form of feedback and it also shows people you care about them and that you have their best interests at heart (Kouzes & Posner, 2002).

360-Degree Feedback for Manager Level and Above

A multirater feedback tool (a 360-degree review) was referred to earlier in this book. This tool is typically administered by either your HR department or your coach and is used for people who have direct reports, not for individual contributors like staff nurses. If you are a director-level nurse or above, you should consider using this tool for your direct reports. The following respondent groups are involved in a 360-degree review: you (the person who is the subject of the 360-degree review), your manager, direct reports, peers, and others. You and your manager would agree on who would be invited to participate in your 360-degree review and their responses would be completely anonymous.

If you were the director of the OB/GYN service, your rater groups would include:

- You (self)

- Your manager

- Your direct reports (all the OB/GYN nurse managers)

- Your peers—which would be some of the other nurse directors in the hospital (those with whom you interact the most)

- Others—might include physicians, OB/GYN staff nurses, other staff who serve on the same committees as you, etc.

LEADERSHIP TIP

This is an excellent source of feedback for the manager level and up, and should be done every two to three years for anyone who has direct reports.

Building a Feedback Culture

Your unit or service has its own subculture that, while part of the larger organizational culture, is a reflection of you and your values. As an authentic leader, you can embed a culture of feedback to help your staff grow. You'll need to do lots of communicating to get them to accept feedback from you and share feedback about others. If staff are going to share their thoughts and observations about their peers (and they don't want to give it to the person themselves) then they must trust you. If you breach their confidence once, you will have to repair it, which may take a while and will set your program back. It should be obvious why it's important to build a trusting culture for feedback and coaching prior to initiating such a process.

References

1. Bing-You, R. G., Bertsch, T., & Thompson, J. A. (1998). "Coaching medical students in receiving effective feedback." *Teaching and Learning in Medicine*, 10(4), 228–231.

2. Carter, J. H. (1992). "Coaching nurses effectively." *Nursing*, 22(10), 109–116.

3. Christiansen, B. (2008). "Good work – How is it recognized by the nurse?" *Journal of Clinical Nursing*, 17, 1645–1651.

4. Kouzes, J. M., & Posner, B. Z. (2002). *The Leadership Challenge* (3rd ed.) San Francisco: Jossey-Bass.

5. Lycette, B., & Herniman, J. (2008). "New goal-setting theory." *Industrial Management*, 50(5), 25–31. Martin, C.A. (2004). "Turn on the staying power." *Nursing Management*, 35(3), 21–27.

6. Martin, C.A. (2004). "Turn on the staying power." *Nursing Management*, 35(3), 21–27.

COACHING FOR DESIRABLE BEHAVIOR

Learning Objectives

After reading this chapter, the reader will be able to:

- ■ Define what is coaching for desirable performance
- ■ List the steps in the coaching process

Your primary responsibility as a manager is to help the organization reach its goals. Managers do this through others. Coaching is one of the most effective development tools you can use to build competence in others. Coaching is an ongoing process to enhance the skills, self-awareness, and self-efficacy of others. In addition, it is used for career development and planning, for processing feedback, and for support during organizational change (Triner & Turner, 2005). Coaching is a skill that can be learned, and it needs to be practiced in order to reach competence that results in changing behavior.

The process of coaching is used extensively in the corporate world and it takes feedback to the next level. You give feedback to others so that they know where they are in relation to goals and expectations. Although coaching includes feedback, it also incorporates another step. Feedback describes actions and the effects of those actions; coaching begins there but then evaluates the appropriateness of the actions and either reinforces what the person is doing well or corrects what the person is doing if the behaviors are ineffective. Where feedback is part one of the process, coaching is part two.

The focus of this chapter is coaching for the reinforcement of effective behaviors (coaching desirable performance). The focus of the next chapter (Chapter 9) is coaching of undesirable performance.

> The focus of this chapter: **Coaching = feedback + reinforcement of good behaviors**

Benefits of Coaching

It is important that people get feedback and coaching on the positive behaviors they are demonstrating so that their desirable behavior will continue, their confidence will grow, their performance will be enhanced, and they will get their needs met (self-esteem, belonging, self-actualization).

What's in it for you? All of those mentioned benefits for your staff, along with higher levels of performance, unit goal achievement, and the possible creation of new peer role models for your staff. As your team takes its performance up a notch, you will feel more self-actualized, and you will be able to focus on other operational and strategic goals.

One of the most commonly cited reasons people give for leaving an organization is a lack of feedback and coaching from managers. We don't like operating in a vacuum and being left alone to struggle through difficult issues; this is especially true for those of us who have the added stress of making life-and-death decisions. Not only does this perceived indifference lead to voluntary turnover (because management "doesn't care"), but also it does little to thwart collective bargaining efforts. Attorneys who counsel hospital administrators on collective bargaining issues cite that training supervisors and managers on sound management skills is one of the most important preventive measures. They claim that managers who know how to treat staff with respect, consistency, and fairness; show concern for staff's well-being; show appreciation; and who can keep lines of communication open will decrease the likelihood of having to entertain a labor issue. Coaching is one way to help prevent turnover and union activity, but it shouldn't be the driving force. You should coach your staff because it's the right thing to do, you care, and you want them to be successful.

Coaching staff to competence

The goal is to move staff along a continuum of competence (see Figure 8.1). When learning a new skill, you are first "unconsciously incompetent." In other words, you don't know what you don't know. That's why feedback is so important; it reveals blind spots in our behavior. After receiving feedback, you move to the stage called "consciously incompetent." Now you are aware of what you don't know. With some coaching, you move to the "consciously competent" state, which is where you work on the new skill. You still need to really think about what you're doing and how you're doing it. After some practice, you become "unconsciously competent."

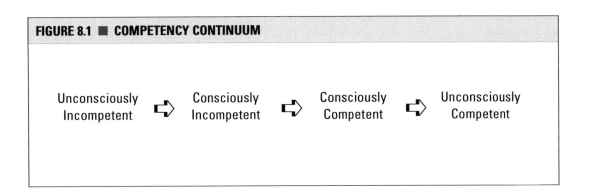

FIGURE 8.1 ■ COMPETENCY CONTINUUM

Unconsciously Incompetent ⇨ Consciously Incompetent ⇨ Consciously Competent ⇨ Unconsciously Competent

If you've ever moved to a big city for a new job and lived 15 miles away from the hospital, you know exactly what this continuum feels like. At first, you don't even know where the hospital is (unconsciously incompetent). So you get directions on how to get there. You try to follow the directions, but miss a turn (consciously incompetent). For the next few days, you closely read the directions and carefully watch the signs and you arrive at your destination (consciously competent). After a few weeks, you don't even think about how to get there, you just drive to the hospital without thinking and without anxiety. You are now unconsciously competent. That's the goal. It takes practice.

Ericsson, Prietula, and Cokely's (2007) *Harvard Business Review* article reviews research describing what it takes for the "making of an expert." They pose that there are three primary ingredients to make anyone truly superior in a particular skill. One of the ingredients is deliberate practice. They note that getting really good at any skill (dancing, golf, tennis, surgery, writing, patient care, communication, leadership, etc.) takes time, practice, and focused concentration to push oneself out of a comfort zone to reach new heights of expertise. Coaching is the second ingredient that must accompany practice in order to provide another perspective and support (the third ingredient) the trainee through what can be a lengthy process to reach levels of excellence. Their thesis is that experts are made, not born. People who desire to attain a high level of functioning tend to be not only open to feedback and coaching, but they seek it out.

The Coaching Process

There can be several variations on the process that you adopt that may range from the informal and spontaneous to the more formal and planned. Either way, the basic ingredients are listed here and should always be incorporated. As with feedback, communicating that coaching is a positive intervention designed to invest in the development of others should precede any change in behavior on your part.

1. **Gather data.** Always start by assessing performance using one of the methods described in Chapter 7: direct observation, a 360-degree review, interviews, record review, etc. Be sure your facts are accurate and double-check if you are unsure. Avoid drawing conclusions if you do not have the entire picture.

2. **Share feedback.** Be sure the person is ready to receive some feedback. If the person is very busy or stressed, it is unlikely that he or she will be able to focus on the situation. This is as important to remember when giving positive feedback and coaching as it is when giving developmental feedback and coaching. Include the person in this discussion, meaning you should be asking for his or her assessment of the situation, action, and effect. This will get him or her to reflect on similar situations in the future when you are not there. Ensure that the feedback you give each person is *balanced*, meaning that you are not always giving either all positive or all critical feedback. While you need not always include both in every coaching conversation, be certain that, overall, your staff gets feedback in both areas.

3. **Ask for input.** After you discuss the situation, action, and effect with coachees, ask whether there is any additional information they can share that would be helpful for you to know. Get them to reflect on how they felt, why they chose that particular action, what thought process led them to choose that action, and how you and they can reinforce that behavior in themselves and others.

4. **Acknowledge the positive behavior**. Express appreciation and share words of praise for a job well done. It is unlikely that you can ever express too much praise and appreciation. Sincerely recognize the efforts coachees took to achieve the outcome. And, when appropriate, mention that you are aware that they stepped out of their comfort zone and took a risk. That kind of encouragement will help them grow and become confident to take additional risks.

5. **Create a development plan.** Since the focus of this chapter is reinforcing desirable behavior, a development plan might not seem necessary. However, staff may become role models for this behavior. The behavior may be a strength that could be leveraged to the rest of the team. The staff could even expand on this strength. You want them to think about what should be done next. Ask open-ended questions at this point if they are having trouble coming up with possible next steps. "The 'art' of coaching is created by letting employees feel that it was they who put the successful plan together, while the 'skill' is in the managers' ability to subconsciously implement (through coaching) the principals [sic] necessary for success" (Mosca, Fazzari & Buzza, 2010). Get them to think.

6. **Follow up.** Because this behavior is positive, support coachee's efforts to continue it. Next time you have a coaching discussion, ask whether they have been able to apply this skill in any other situations and find out how it worked.

7. **Reevaluate.** Assess whether this behavior is still being demonstrated through one of the data collection methods mentioned in the last chapter. If it is, congratulate coachees on this success. You may set new bars of achievement for them to stretch their skills by giving additional responsibilities. However, you may be able to coach them to yet a new level, if it is appropriate for this behavior. And the process starts over. Since we are always evolving and growing (since few people become fully self-actualized), there may always be coaching, even on areas that are strengths. You may even need to find employees a new coach for this particular skill, someone who is more skilled than you are. At some point, you'll be able to stop reinforcement of this particular behavior since it will have become second nature (unconsciously competent).

EXAMPLE 1

Courtney is one of your nurse leaders who is fairly new in the role. One of her goals is to become proficient at recognizing and hiring new talent for the unit. You give her some background on the hiring process, have her observe you interviewing a couple of times, and then ask her to ask the interview questions for one competency while you listen. She does a great job in the way she asks questions; her nonverbal communication is good and puts the candidate at ease, and she deftly gets the information necessary to evaluate the candidate's fitness for that competency. She is able to elicit a situation, action, and result for two examples for the one competency. Here is an example of coaching this desirable behavior and what it might sound like:

Gather data

You observed Courtney during the interview. You made note of the questions she asked, her nonverbal communication, and the effect it had on the candidate.

Share feedback

You: Courtney, you asked some excellent questions and gathered some very pertinent information about the candidate's past performance. You seemed relaxed, which helped to relax him.

Ask for input

You: Tell me about what you gathered.

Courtney: Well, when I was asking him about his organizing skills, he was able to give me the example of how he handled the three postops who returned to his floor within a short period of time. He mentioned that he prioritized the care that needed to be given to each patient depending on the relative stability of each patient, that he elicited the help of the patient care technician to do vitals, which he checked, and was then able to administer the treatments and meds that were required for each. He said it was hectic, but that all patients did well and remained stable. Then he gave me the second example.

You: How do you think the candidate was feeling during your interaction with him? What did you observe?

EXAMPLE 1 (CONT.)

Courtney: He seemed pretty comfortable, although he had some trouble coming up with the second example.

You: What did you do when that happened?

Courtney: Let's see, I guess that's when I said it was okay to take a minute to think of another example. I think I said that I know it can be difficult sometimes to recall situations like this, especially during an interview. I smiled.

Acknowledge the positive behavior

You: Exactly. You did a really great job asking the questions per the interview guide and I agree that you were able to get all the information needed to evaluate his candidacy on that competency by asking follow-up questions. Do you remember when you said, "That must have been overwhelming, what did you do?" You empathized with him and probed for his action. Great job! You also noticed his body language when he got a bit flustered trying to come up with another example. You put him at ease by smiling and, again, empathizing with him. I'm very impressed with the way you handled that part of the interview and I appreciate your attention to detail.

Create the development plan

You: What do you feel would help you continue to build your interviewing skills?

Courtney: Well, I guess I should do this again.

You: I agree. How would you feel about opening the interview in addition to interviewing for two competencies?

Courtney: I'd like to try that.

You: Great. Before my next interview, you and I will sit down and go over the elements of opening an interview. You can role-play with me to be sure you're comfortable. Is there anything else you need?

Courtney: I don't think so. But thank you for helping me with this. I enjoyed it.

EXAMPLE 1 (CONT.)

Follow-up

Follow-up in this case would be for you to provide Courtney with another interview experience and some instruction and role-playing. If she were at the point where she would be interviewing on her own, you would follow up with her to see how it went and you might even ask the candidate how he/she felt the interview went and whether he/she had any feedback for Courtney.

Reevaluate

As you observe Courtney during the next interview, you will reevaluate how she does asking the competency-based questions, then give her feedback and coaching. But the process will start all over since she will be opening the interview for the first time and will need feedback and coaching on that.

In this case, you got her to assess the situation and you gave specific feedback later after she had thought about how she did. Since this example showed a coaching session for desirable behavior, notice that you offered not only to have her repeat what she had done well (she'll need some repetition on this skill before she becomes unconsciously competent) but also to take the bar up a notch to stretch her skills in a new area.

EXAMPLE 2

Coaching can also happen spontaneously as the situation dictates. Brenda is a charge nurse on an orthopedic floor. While reviewing the postop notes for a particular patient, she noted that the patient's routine meds were not reordered by the surgeon. It took her quite a while to reconcile all the medications and as a result, other patients didn't get the attention that they needed. When the surgeon comes onto the unit, Brenda asks to speak to him. You, the nurse manager, overhear what turns into a heated conversation. Brenda tells him about the meds that need to be ordered. He gets very defensive and raises his voice, saying that he is so busy. He starts to complain about the primary physician, claiming it was her job to order the meds. Brenda brings the conversation back to the issue at hand and tells him that he is the one who needed to write these orders. She does not let him overpower her; she holds her ground. In the end, he agrees that he will write the orders. There is mutual agreement about the situation.

Gather data

You observed the interaction.

Share feedback

You: Brenda, you did a great job with what looked like was going to be a difficult conversation. First of all, you noticed an error by thoroughly assessing the situation. You confronted the physician about an oversight on his part. When he tried to escalate the conversation and divert attention away from himself, you held your ground and pursued until he agreed to write the orders. In the end, the patient will get the critical meds that he needs.

Ask for input

You: How did you feel about this interaction?

Brenda: Well, I don't like confronting people, but there really wasn't any choice here since he had to write orders for all the patient's meds, not just the postop meds. I didn't like it when he raised his voice, but I hung in there.

You: What did you say to calm him down? Do you remember?

Brenda: I think I said something like "I understand you are busy, but this is an important matter."

Acknowledge the positive behavior

You: Exactly, and you maintained a calm, controlled demeanor. You didn't let him escalate you. And the matter was resolved because of what you did and how you did it. Well done. I'm very proud of you.

---

104 **Lead! Becoming an Effective Coach and Mentor to Your Nursing Staff**

© 2010 HCPro, Inc.

This example probably wouldn't require a formal development plan; however, you would want to try to observe Brenda in a similar situation again to reinforce good communication skills. You would want to reevaluate to be sure the skill was continued.

Skills and Behavior of Good Coaches

Good coaches should have the following skills:

- Interpersonal and relationship-building skills

- Emotional intelligence:

    - "[A]bilities such as being able to motivate oneself and persist in the face of frustrations;

    - to control impulse and delay gratification;

    - to regulate one's moods and keep distress from swamping the ability to think;

    - to empathize and to hope." (Goleman, 1995)

- Communication:

    - Verbal

    - Nonverbal

- Accountability

- Patience

- Flexibility

- Goal setting; also able to monitor and assess progress toward goal (Carter, 1992)

Behaviors of a good coach:

- Role models the effective behavior

- Gives clear, direct praise and criticism (Doucette, 2007)

- Guides coachee to release their own potential

- Shares coping skills

- Is credible; builds confidence

- Asks great questions to make the coachee think; good coaches don't prescribe solutions (Whitmore, 2002), they guide the coachee to "connect the dots" themselves

- Listens

- Holds coachee accountable

- Sets ground rules: confidentiality, ethics, commitment

- Provides support

As a coach, you always want to get the coachees to reflect on the situation themselves. When things get tense, and emotions escalate, people are not always as aware of their behavior as they should be. If you are in a position to observe a behavior, asking coachees to recount what they did will help them build awareness and help embed the practice of reflection. Figure 8.2 contains tips on what to say to staff members to encourage them to reflect on their actions and the effects of their actions.

Many people find it exhilarating to coach and develop someone else to reach their potential. Your staff are your greatest asset and you will excel or fail based on the level of their skill and engagement in their jobs, in the organization, and in you. Coaching others to reach and sustain positive behaviors is one of the most rewarding aspects of any manager's job. Receiving coaching shows care, trust, and support, and is one of the most rewarding parts of any employee's job as well. Make it a focus to get good at coaching and do it—a lot.

FIGURE 8.2 ■ QUESTIONS TO ASK STAFF MEMBERS

To encourage staff members to reflect on their actions and the effects of their actions, ask open-ended questions that start with "what," "how," or "which," such as:

- What precipitated the action?
- What were the circumstances that led you to do that?
- What reaction did you receive?
- How did you react?
- What was your tone of voice?
- Which factors did you consider?
- What other actions have you tried in similar situations?
- What was the effect on the other person?
- How did you make that decision?

Try to get at staff members' motivation for the action:

- What were you feeling when you said that?
- What were you thinking might happen?

Avoid "why" questions. Instead of asking, "Why did you do that?," ask:

- What factors did you consider?

Avoid leading questions such as "You must have felt great after that interaction." Instead, ask:

- How did you feel after that interaction?

Let coachees describe how they felt. Even in positive coaching scenarios, you'll be surprised how often coachees feel different from the way we think they will.

References

1. Carter, J. H. (1992). "Coaching nurses effectively." *Nursing*, 22(10), 109–116.

2. Doucette, J. (2007). "A man's world: Coach new nurses for success." *Men in Nursing*, 2(2), 56.

3. Ericsson, K. A., Prietula, M. J., & Cokely, E. T. (2007). "The making of an expert." *Harvard Business Review*, 85(7/8), 114–121.

4. Goleman, D. (1995). *Emotional Intelligence: Why It Can Matter More Than IQ.* New York: Bantam Books.

5. Hooijberg, R., & Lane, N. (2009). "Using multisource feedback coaching effectively in executive education." *Academy of Management Learning and Education*, 8(4), 483–493.

6. Mosca, J. B., Fazzari, A., & Buzza, J. (2010). "Coaching to win: A systematic approach to achieving productivity through coaching." *Journal of Business & Economics Research*, 8(5), 115–130.

7. St. John-Brooks, K. (2010). "Moral support." *Coaching Ethics*, 5(1), 48–51.

8. Stoltzfus, T. (2008). *Coaching Questions: A Coach's Guide to Powerful Asking Skills.* Pegasus Creative Arts.

9. Triner, J., & Turner, S. (2005). "Professional coaches and employee assistance practitioners serving corporate and individual clients." *Journal of Workplace Behavioral Health*, 21(2), 1–14.

10. Whitmore, J. (2002). *Coaching for Performance* (3rd ed.). London: Nicholas Brealey Publishing.

CHAPTER 9

CONSTRUCTIVE COACHING

Learning Objectives

After reading this chapter, the reader will be able to:

- Explain the steps to take in a constructive coaching scenario

- Identify the elements of a development plan

Constructive coaching to improve skill level is critical, as coaching is one of the most effective ways to change behavior. It is the method by which you support someone through the process of changing ineffective behavior to effective behavior. If you have built your culture to represent this type of coaching as helpful and supportive, rather than critical and punitive, then it will be viewed in a positive light. People should not be threatened by constructive coaching nor by having a development plan. Everyone needs to have a development plan, even if they are "superstars." Your superstars still need to be continually learning and continually challenged, and everyone needs to be sure they are leveraging their skills and continuing to build on their strengths.

Importance of Constructive Coaching

For people to listen to and accept your feedback and coaching, they need to have open and receptive minds. They cannot be in a fearful state, because they will not be able to hear you (literally) if their bodies are preparing for fight or flight. Setting the tone for constructive coaching scenarios is something to think about before you initiate the discussion.

A culture that supports feedback and coaching will make almost every constructive coaching conversation one that does not make others feel defensive. Your staff will realize that the reason you are taking the time to have this discussion with them is to help them be better professionally, as nurses, teammates, and colleagues, and to help them grow to use their skills to the fullest. The conversation will not have a negative effect; people will not feel they have been chastised. Rather, it will have a positive effect and they will leave feeling a little humbled (no one is perfect) but also empowered. They will now have the tools to perform at a higher level the next time this situation arises. That will give them confidence. How could they not be appreciative about that? The culture you establish and the delivery of this kind of conversation make all the difference.

Examples of behaviors that may require constructive coaching include incomplete charting; taking too long to chart; errors; accidents; not tending to patients in appropriate time; inappropriate attitude and actions toward patients or colleagues; bullying others, tardiness; excessive absences; lacking skills or awareness of standards; and failing to achieve goals, objectives, or expectations. The constructive coaching process not only helps you to change these behaviors, but also helps you get to the cause of the behaviors. Reasons for poor performance can include personal issues (domestic violence, family or personal health issues, substance abuse, fatigue, and shift changes) or organizational issues (inadequate training, poor communication of policies or standards, poor role models or preceptors, discomfort with new technology, poor management and support, and bullying) (Ellis, 2008). Having this discussion will help you get to the cause of the behavior so that you can create a perfect solution, when necessary. The problem may be systemic and go beyond just this one person.

Delivering Constructive Feedback and Coaching

The process is the same as that described in Chapter 8.

1. **Gather data.** Your data-collecting process may be methodical and planned or it may be spontaneous, such as when you walk on the unit and observe a behavior that is not consistent with the goals, expectations, or clinical standards. Regardless, as before, be sure that you have as complete a picture as possible, but don't wait to have a discussion until you have every detail. If the observed behavior is egregious, such as when a safety violation has occurred, it needs to be addressed very quickly. Staff can fill you in on the details during the discussion.

2. **Share feedback.** Most of the time, it will be appropriate to open your conversation with some appreciation for all the fine things that the person does. As you know, most humans need and deserve respect and appreciation, so be sure to open this conversation in a positive, caring manner.

   You need your feedback to be as timely as possible, so having the discussion as soon as possible after you observed the behavior is very important to maximize the impact and result of the discussion. No one wants to think that you are gathering a file full of critical feedback to share during a performance appraisal discussion. That would not be a trust-building activity. Never hoard feedback of any kind.

   When sharing feedback, you can choose to share it either directly yourself, have the coachee tell you what happened, or use a combination. You should at least begin by commenting on what you observed: the situation and the coachee's actions. Asking the coachee to describe the effect of his or her behavior is a good way to stimulate reflection so that the person can start to get into the habit of doing this on his or her own in the future.

Lead! Becoming an Effective Coach and Mentor to Your Nursing Staff   **111**

© 2010 HCPro, Inc.

When sharing feedback, the delivery is more important than the message itself (Goleman & Boyatzis, 2008). You want to frame the discussion in a positive, helpful manner and keep your emotions in check. By maintaining a positive, professional, and helping demeanor, you will hold coachees' attention and respect. They will be more accepting of what you have to say.

3. **Ask for input.** At this point in the discussion, you might ask the coachee about his or her motivation for the particular behavior as well as for any other details about the situation about which you could not be aware. Try to dig a big deeper, when necessary. Try to determine why the person did what he or she did. The answer might be something as simple as "I didn't know that I was doing that incorrectly" or it might be something more profound like "I was afraid to say anything." The answer will heighten your awareness about the possible systemic nature of the problem.

4. **Coach for desired behavior and desired effect**. Since we are talking about less-than-effective behavior in this chapter, acknowledge that to the coachees. They need to leave the discussion being very clear on what they did that was ineffective vs. what optimal behavior looks like. Empathize when appropriate.

   Either describe for them (or get them to tell you):

   - What a desired behavior would have been in that situation

   - What the effect of the desired behavior would have likely been

5. **Create a development plan.** Get coachees to think about what they will do differently the next time they are in a similar situation. Again, whether a written development plan is necessary depends on the nature of the situation. If one of your expectations is that everybody takes responsibility for unit cleanliness and you see one of your staff walk over a piece of paper on the floor, you

will give this staff member some feedback and coaching, but you probably don't need a development plan unless you notice that this behavior continues. However, if the issue is more significant, such as delayed or missing record-keeping, or having a heated discussion with a colleague in a patient area, you will probably want to create a development plan. This plan will describe exactly what the person needs to do and by when to demonstrate effective behavior.

6. **Follow up.** You can follow up by asking coachees how they are doing with the particular behavior (not with the piece of paper on the floor, but with the more substantial behaviors). Find out whether they have had the opportunity to use the more effective behavior. If their development plan called for them to have a conversation with another staff member, follow up to be sure the conversation happened, and to determine how it went and whether they need any additional coaching from you about it. If they haven't had the conversation and it is an experience that you can provide for them, then do that. You will not be able to orchestrate an experience for every behavior that your staff might be working on, nor would you want to. However, do it when you can. For example, there may be clinical situations that you can place them in to reinforce a behavior, etc.

Following up demonstrates that this is an important issue to you and it should also be to them. If you don't follow up, agreed-upon subsequent actions may not happen. If the person is having difficulty, it gives you the opportunity to *offer your support.*

7. **Reevaluate.** Whether you reevaluate via a formal mechanism (360-degree review, interviews, etc.) or by merely observing, be sure to get some data to determine whether new behaviors are being demonstrated effectively. Let coachees know what your reevaluation results are so that they know they are on the right track. Express appreciation for their efforts and progress.

Create a Development Plan

Create a development plan that works for your hospital. Keep it simple and concise so that it gets used. Some elements that a typical development plan should include are:

- Identification of the skill or competency under focus

- Activities to be completed; dates of completion for each activity

- Benefits to the coachee, unit, organization

- Demonstration or application of skill or competency (how, when, and who will observe)

Everyone should have a development plan since everyone has areas in which they can grow, even if these are already areas of strength.

How to involve staff in the process

Keeping your staff involved in the coaching process helps ensure buy-in and continuance of the new behaviors. Whenever possible, ask them open-ended questions to get them thinking and coming up with ideas and possibilities. The more they can re-create the problem, its antecedents, and the solution, the more self-awareness and other-awareness they will have. As they improve their awareness, they will be more understanding of other people's behaviors (good and bad) and will have more confidence in their abilities to react to them in an effective manner. It will help them to pause before launching into an ineffective behavior.

Look back at the open-ended questions in Figure 8.2. These are the types of questions to use to keep the coachees involved in the process. You really want them to be involved in the development planning process. If you don't have their agreement on the steps to take and on the timeline, the process is unlikely to be done. Get coachees generating options and ideas and thinking through the rationale behind them. Involvement will help the change stick.

For example, one of your goals is to reassess pain within 30 minutes after the adminis-
tration of pain medication. After auditing charts, you notice that one of your nurses is
not meeting the goal for pain reassessment within the allotted time frame (Step 1:
Gather data).

What is one open-ended question you could ask him or her during each of the next six
steps of the coaching process?

   2. Share feedback_____

   3. Ask for input_____

   4. Coach for desired behavior_____

   5. Create a development plan_____

   6. Follow up_____

   7. Reevaluate _____

There is no one perfect answer; here are some options:

   2. **Share feedback:** "As I was looking though your patient's chart, I noticed that
      you did not reevaluate pain within 30 minutes of giving the pain med. What
      is the reason that we want to reevaluate pain medication within 30 minutes
      of administration?" This type of question might sound obvious, but it will get
      him or her thinking about the effects of his or her behavior and remind him or
      her of the importance of this policy. If he or she is new, there is the possibility
      that he or she forgot or was unaware of the policy.

   3. **Ask for input:** "What are some factors that prevented you from reassessing
      these patients?" This might help you identify the reasons that he or she is not
      reassessing in a timely manner: poor time management, inadequate training,
      poor attention to detail, distractions on the unit, personal issues, etc. Assuming

he or she is aware of the policy, questions like this one will help you get to the root cause.

4. **Coach for desired behavior:** "What actions will you take next time you have a patient who requires pain meds? How are you going to be sure that you are able to do this? What are some of the benefits of reassessing these patients?"

5. **Create a development plan:** "How will you ensure that you do this in the future with all of your pain-medicated patients? What steps would be helpful to you? What support do you need?"

6. **Follow up:** "How is your pain med assessment going? How are you able to reassess with the consistency that we discussed? What has changed?"

7. **Reevaluate:** "I just completed a chart audit on your pain-medicated patients. What do you think I found?"

You would never ask all these questions; this is not an interrogation. Rather, you want to balance your questions with your observations. In most cases, managers are likely to do most of the talking about their observations, although in reality asking reflection questions is much better for the coachee and you, even if the process takes a little bit more time.

Barriers to Coaching Effectiveness

According to a study by Hooijberg and Lane (2009), the number one cited obstacle to coaching effectiveness was the coachees themselves. They mentioned attitude, personality, staying committed, habits, and reverting to old behaviors as reasons that the coaching results were not as spectacular as they could have been. The second most frequently cited reason was lack of time for the coachee to implement the development plan. Together, these two reasons made up more than 50% of the responses in the study.

One of the first questions to ask potential coachees is whether they are open to coaching and committed to doing what needs to be done to change behavior and change results. It is clear from the research cited earlier that without the commitment, any behavior that might occur will likely slide back if it is not reinforced by you or by another coach, until coachees have reached the "unconsciously competent" level. Therefore, just because the person uses the correct behavior once, do not assume that it has become part of his or her DNA. The coachee will need reinforcement from you for a while, until you are reasonably sure "it has stuck." Behavior change takes time; be sure to give that to your staff. The only exception to this is, of course, anything that is potentially life threatening; those behaviors need to change stat and will be covered in the next chapter, on confrontation.

Leave staff feeling good about themselves, you, and the organization

As you close a constructive coaching discussion, be sure to let the person know that you appreciate all his or her efforts and good work that he or she does. You also appreciate his or her open attitude in discussing the present situation. Again, offer your support in helping the person achieve his or her goal and express your confidence in his or her ability to develop. Let the person know that he or she is valued by the organization and by his or her patients, team, and you.

Closing the discussion in a positive manner will help your staff look at developmental feedback as a positive rather than a negative interaction so that trust can continue to build.

E X A M P L E

Jean is in charge of the unit on the day that the chair of the department and one of the residents decide to get into a heated discussion about the resident's vacation request. They are right in the middle of a patient care area and seem oblivious that other staff members and patients can hear their ranting. You, the nurse manager, are able to hear the interaction. Jean walks over to them and says:

Jean: Let me remind you that you are in a patient area and not only are your voices raised, which is bothersome in itself, but no one cares about your vacation squabble, so take it outside.

Resident: (in a sharp and condescending tone) Who appointed you general?

Jean feels her BP rise and storms out of the area and into her nurse manager's office.

Jean: (visibly angry) Did you hear that? How dare that little brat say that to me?

You: Yes, I heard it (gathering data) and I can see you're upset. You really let her get to you. Take a deep breath and let's talk about what happened there. Describe the moods of all the players.

Jean: Well, the resident was upset since she wasn't able to get the vacation week that she wanted, so she was giving the chair a piece of her mind. It was pretty obnoxious of her, but I guess she feels some entitlement since her father is on staff here.

You: I imagine so. Do you recall what you said to them?

Jean: I told them to take their discussion away from the area.

You: Yes, and you also said that no one cares about her vacation. What effect do you think that might have had on her already agitated state? (sharing feedback and getting her input)

Jean: Well, that last comment probably didn't help the situation.

You: That's true. What prompted you to say it?

Jean: I don't like her attitude anyway. I think she is a spoiled brat who was born with a silver spoon in her mouth.

Lead! Becoming an Effective Coach and Mentor to Your Nursing Staff

EXAMPLE (CONT.)

You: So your resentment of her entered into this?

Jean: I guess so.

You: When you have a goal such as you had—to get them to move their conversation—it probably doesn't help to bring personal opinions into the conversation. It would have been a good time to focus on what you wanted—them moving their discussion—without adding to the emotions. Does that make sense? (coaching for desired behavior)

Jean: Yes.

You: When she made that crack to you about being a "general," what did you do?

Jean: I was so mad, I came in here.

You: Was that effective behavior?

Jean: No, but I was too upset to talk to them.

You: She pushed your buttons, but you chose to leave rather than to see that they got off the unit. What could you have said and done at that point had you stayed?

Jean: I guess I could have ignored her stupid comment, looked at the chair, who should know better than to let an immature resident talk to him that way on the unit, and said something like, "Are you going to lower your voices or move this conversation?"

You: That would have worked. What would that comment and behavior from you have communicated to them?

Jean: That I'm not going to be intimidated by a resident, that I can hold my ground and do what is right for the patients and staff.

You: Exactly. How would you have felt about yourself then vs. how you felt coming in here all upset?

Jean: I would have felt strong and empowered to hold my own with them instead of giving my power to them.

You: Precisely. Next time, you have a plan. Stay and finish the conversation in a professional manner despite how juvenile they might be acting. Good debrief, Jean. Thanks. Let me know how it goes next time.

Getting staff to change behavior and take risks

The previous example shows your understanding and support in a highly charged situation. By helping the staff members think through the best behavior and the benefits of that vs. reacting in an emotional and ineffective manner, you can start to get them to be aware of their emotions and the emotions of others, to make a decision on the best course of action to get the outcome they want, and to commit to taking risks or at least breaking out of a comfort zone (e.g., fleeing a highly charged situation). Many people, men and women alike, are conflict avoidant. Fleeing from conflict rarely helps one achieve his or her goals, or build stronger relationships. In fact, addressing conflict usually helps to build deeper relationships and trust.

Coaching best practices

Coaching takes time; don't expect results to happen overnight. The change in behavior is a function of the difficulty of the skill, the frequency of the coaching sessions, and the frequency of the opportunities to demonstrate the skill.

Figure 9.1 is an example of confronting a difficult colleague versus starting an IV.

FIGURE 9.1 ■ DIFFICULTY OF COACHING VERSUS TECHNICAL TASK		
Situation	**Difficult conversation**	**Starting an IV**
Skill difficulty/complexity	Complex	Less complex
Frequency of coaching sessions	Depends	Depends
Frequency of practice sessions	Infrequent	Frequent
Time to embed new skill	More time	Less time

The more complex the skill and the more infrequent the coaching sessions, the fewer opportunities to practice and therefore the longer it will take to see a change in behavior and the longer it will take to embed the behavior in the DNA.

Consider letting your staff know what is on *your* development plan. This way, they may feel open to give you some feedback on the skill on which you are working, if you invite them to do so. Talk about a trust-building behavior!

References

1. Ellis, J. (2008). "Managing performance." *Nursing Management —UK,* 15(1), 28–33.

2. Goleman, D., & Boyatzis, R. (2008). "Social intelligence and the biology of leadership." *Harvard Business Review*, 86(9), 74–81.

3. Hooijberg, R., & Lane, N. (2009). "Using multisource feedback coaching effectively in executive education." *Academy of Management Learning and Education*, 8(4), 483–493.

MANAGING CONFRONTATIONS

Learning Objectives

After reading this chapter, the reader will be able to:

- Explain how a confrontation discussion differs from a constructive coaching discussion

- Explain the circumstances under which a confrontation discussion should occur

"All problems become smaller if you don't dodge them, but confront them."
—*Admiral William F. Halsey*

Everybody has worked for an organization where disruptive behavior or lazy workers are allowed to continue their ineffective behavior unabated, enjoying all the benefits of employment that the diligent workers enjoy. Coworkers notice. There is whispering. People avoid the disruptive or lazy workers. The conscientious, hard workers grow resentful. Productivity and morale drop; errors are made. Employee engagement and patient satisfaction scores drop; turnover rises. Problems get bigger if not addressed.

What Is a Confrontation?

People need to be confronted about behaviors that are not consistent with the goals and expectations that you set forth. Your inability to address these situations makes you look weak and fearful. People don't tend to follow, respect, and trust a feeble leader who has low "street cred" because he or she can't face the challenges. Your ignoring unacceptable behavior signals your tacit approval of it. How is the staff supposed to feel empowered to confront others and have difficult conversations if you don't?

How do I know when to give constructive feedback and coaching, and when to confront?

It becomes time to confront people when they have been coached on a particular behavior and there has not been enough progress on that behavior. How much is enough coaching? It depends on the seriousness of the behavior. If you are coaching someone on a particular skill, you will likely give the person plenty of time to develop that skill. If, however, there is an expectation with which a staff member is not complying—for example, how to treat other staff—you might need to coach them only once or twice before you begin the disciplinary process, which starts with a confrontation.

A confrontation discussion needs to happen:

- After the person has received adequate coaching and there has not been a satisfactory degree of improvement in performance or behavior; or

- If the person has violated a policy or a standard or expectation, which makes that person's behavior unsafe or disruptive

A confrontation discussion differs from a constructive coaching discussion in two very important ways:

- The behavior in question *must change* immediately

- The confrontation discussion *includes consequences* if the behavior were to happen again

Examples of consequences include verbal warning, written warning, suspension, and termination. When you get to this point in working with someone, be sure to involve your human resources (HR) representative. Whether you are working in a union or nonunion environment, you have to consider possible legal ramifications, and you want to be sure you are in line with the policies of your HR department. Involve them sooner rather than later. They are an extremely valuable resource who will help you stay out of court.

Why managers avoid confrontation

Almost no one enjoys confrontations with others. Naturally, most managers prefer calm, harmonious personal and professional relationships. The primary reason these types of discussions are avoided is *fear*. Everyone has some degree of fear and it is human nature to circumvent it if at all possible.

So what is everyone afraid of? Here are a few possibilities:

- Humiliation
  - What if the person turns the discussion on me and starts complaining about *my* shortcomings? What if he or she makes a scene?

- Retaliation
  - What might he or she do to "get back at me"?
  - What if the person files a lawsuit? See case study discussed in the article "Minimizing the risks of discriminatory suits when terminating poor per-formers," 2001.

- Emotional outbursts
  - What if the person starts to cry or get angry and shout?

- Loss of self-identity
  - If this doesn't go well, will others view me as incompetent?

- Rejection
  - What if I inadvertently hurt the person's feelings or he or she hurts mine?
  - What if he or she leaves?

You need to face your fears. Think through the examples of fears listed previously and answer the questions that are listed. This exercise will help you to realize that the likelihood and consequences of your fears being realized are outweighed by the damage done of not addressing the problem. You will look much stronger confronting someone, even if the person overreacts, gets emotional, etc., than you will if you look the other way. Also, if you carefully prepare for this discussion using the process discussed later, your odds of having it go well will soar. Once you have had few of these successful discussions, you will become confident and your fears will diminish. Preparation is key. Winging it could be a disaster.

If you avoid having the confrontation discussion, your stress builds and instead of having a planned discussion, your comments come out spontaneously, indirectly, or sideways in the form of:

- **"Flight,"** which includes avoidance behaviors such as sarcasm and negative nonverbal communication (rolling of eyes, shaking head, etc.); or

- **"Fight"** behaviors, as when you have had enough and you lose your temper or even just speak in a sharp tone with ill-chosen words

Dealing with Emotions

You must always remain calm and in control of *your* emotions. In dealing with *their* emotions, expect that they may become uncomfortable, which is okay. Treat others with respect to help prevent outbursts.

Prepare, prepare, prepare

Review your records, check your facts, and check with HR if necessary—and it usually is. Know what you are going to say. This meeting should not be a long, drawn-out meeting. Your comments should be succinct and to the point, and your words well chosen. Your words should be clear and allow no room for misinterpretation. One way to ensure that is to use emphatic language (e.g., "This will happen") instead of ambiguous language (e.g., "This might happen"). Although you should not read a script to an employee, you might write down your words and practice saying them aloud. These types of conversations are critical and you want to take all measures possible to ensure that they are not misconstrued.

Plan what you will say and also put some time into thinking about how you will execute the dialogue. As discussed earlier, 93% of all communication is nonverbal, so consider the type of nonverbal communication tactics that you will employ. If you are having a serious conversation with someone, it is imperative to match your nonverbal style to your words. For a serious matter, you must look and sound serious.

Carefully consider the following prior to having a confrontation discussion with someone, realizing that even if he or she gets upset, you must remain cool, calm, and collected. Consider first your visual impact: posture, hand gestures, facial expression, eye contact. If you tend to fidget when stressed, plan to sit still. Fidgeting connotes stress, which does not give you a powerful demeanor. If you tend to avert eye contact when stressed, be sure you maintain good eye contact in this discussion. You want to look in control of yourself and the discussion. Your voice makes up the other nonverbal communication factor that you have to think about, and it includes pace, tone, intonations, and volume. Plan on having your voice sound as serious as the discussion. You don't want to come across as harsh but you don't want to sound animated and happy. Your pace should be slow, your tone low, intonations should be kept to a minimum, and your volume should be moderate.

The Process: For Direct Reports or Colleagues

The process is the same whether you are confronting a direct report or a colleague, with one exception. You can only start the disciplinary process with those who report to you. Therefore, your discussion of consequences if the behavior does not change will be different for colleagues—or may even be absent.

Conduct this meeting in a private area. Consider inviting another leader to be with you to observe and help recall comments made so that your postmeeting documentation is complete. The process for confronting a direct report or a colleague is as follows:

- Reaffirm the purpose of the meeting

- Summarize any past discussions about the behavior in question; be very brief

- State your intention for this discussion

- Describe his or her behavior

- Describe the impact it is having

- State that this behavior must change and describe the consequences of not changing it

- Reiterate the desired behavior

- Ask for questions

- Ask him or her to reiterate what you have said

- Offer your support

Document, document, document

Documentation is the most-cited reason that employment lawsuits are won or lost (Williams, 2002). Your HR department should have a process that requires a specific document to be filled out at the time of the discussion, with the employee acknowledging by signing that the discussion occurred at a certain time on a certain date.

The last step is to follow up. Be certain that if the behavior happens again, you continue with the stated process. Don't look the other way or you will be communicating that you are not sincere about this and that the behavior really is okay even though it is not.

EXAMPLE 1

Direct Report

Use of cell phones on the unit: One of your staff nurses uses her cell phone on the unit to make personal phone calls. She has been reminded of the policy and has already received a verbal warning from you. But you have seen her using her cell phone again today. You ask her to meet you in your office at 3:30 to talk about the phone use.

- Reaffirm the purpose of the meeting. "We're here today to discuss your use of your cell phone on the unit during working hours."

- Summarize any past discussions about the behavior in question. Be very brief. "We've talked about this in the past, the policy is clear to you, and during our last discussion you received a verbal warning."

- State your intention for this discussion. "My intention here is to help you adhere to the policy since you are a good nurse and I want you to stay with us. Our patients come first and cell phones are not permitted in patient areas."

- Describe his or her behavior. "However, earlier today, I observed you using your cell phone on the unit again."

- Describe the impact it is having. "It is disruptive to others and it distracts you from your patient care responsibilities."

- State that this behavior must change and describe the consequences of not changing it. "You must stop using your cell phone while on the unit immediately. Today, you will receive a written warning. If it happens again, further disciplinary action will be taken up to and including termination."

- Reiterate the desired behavior. "While at work, I expect your attention to be on your patients and helping your teammates as needed and fulfilling any other work-related obligations."

- Ask for questions. "Is there anything I have said that is unclear to you? Do you have any questions for me?"

- Ask him or her to reiterate what you have said. "I'd like you to reiterate what I have said to you today."

- Offer your support. "As always, I am here to help support and develop you and the rest of the staff. Please come see me if you need to discuss anything with me."

EXAMPLE 2

Direct Report

The employee in this scenario has been late on a number of occasions (in violation of whatever your policy states) and you have documented those occasions of tardiness. Now you have to move to a confrontation and start the disciplinary process.

- Reaffirm the purpose of the meeting. "We're here today to discuss your tardiness this morning and review the consequences that will occur if this behavior continues."

- Summarize any past discussions about the behavior in question. Be brief. "As you know, you were late on (X) recent occasions. We documented these occurrences."

- State your intention for this discussion. "My intention is to help you understand how important it is for you to be on time, support you in doing that, and to review consequences if this continues."

- Describe his or her behavior. "Today you were late again."

- Describe the impact it is having. "This affects the rest of the team, who have to cover your patients until you arrive. This is unfair to them and jeopardizes patient care."

- State that this behavior must change and describe the consequences of not chang-ing it. "From now on, I expect you to arrive on time for your shift. The next time you are tardy, you will get a written warning."

- Reiterate the desired behavior and ask for agreement. "Can I expect you to be on time from now on?"

- Ask for questions. "Is anything that I've said today unclear to you? Do you have any comments or questions?"

- Ask him or her to reiterate what you have said. "I'd like you to reiterate what I have said to you today."

- Offer your support. "Know that I'm always here to help support you in any way I can to help you give the best patient care possible."

As you can see from the previous two examples, these types of discussion are typically brief and require little interaction. Although the need for employee discussion is minimal, the person must be given the opportunity to ask questions or clarify any misinformation. When you review these types of interactions with HR, be sure to ask when the employee assistance program (EAP) should be offered to the employee.

EXAMPLE 3

Colleague

A fellow nurse manager made critical comments about your staff in front of the other nurse managers on the service. Notice that in this case, although the process is similar, not all steps are necessary or appropriate.

- Reaffirm the purpose of the meeting. "Can I talk to you for a minute? I'd like to discuss a situation that happened today."

- Summarize any past discussions about the behavior in question. Be very brief.

- State your intention for this discussion. "As you know, I enjoy our working relationship and I want to keep our relationship mutually supportive and open. That's why I feel it's important to mention this to you."

- Describe his or her behavior. "This morning at our nurse manager meeting, you mentioned that during yesterday's conference call, my staff 'looked bad.' I guess you meant that they appeared to be unprepared for the call. Is that what you meant?"

- Describe the impact it is having. "Although I welcome feedback on my staff, I felt a little embarrassed by your comment and surprised that you hadn't said anything to me ahead of time in private about your observation."

- N/A: State that this behavior must change and describe the consequences.

- Reiterate the desired behavior. "In the future, I'd really appreciate it if you have any critical feedback about my staff that you share it with me privately instead of in front of the entire group. I'll do the same for you."

- Ask for questions. "Is that agreeable to you?"

- Ask him or her to reiterate what you have said.

- Offer your support.

EXAMPLE 4

Colleague

Sometimes confrontations with colleagues happen spontaneously, as in the example that follows. In this case, you will not have time to prepare and need to think quickly on your feet. Having this amended process in your mind will help you know how to react to these spontaneous, often highly charged situations.

Anything like this ever happen to you?

You observe Dr. "Alpha," who comes onto your unit to check on a patient only to discover that _____ (you fill in the blank) hasn't been done (medication, treatment, blood work, etc.). He gets irate and demands to see the nurse caring for his patient. He proceeds to speak to her abruptly in a loud voice, not bothering to stop and listen to find out why _____ has been delayed. You overhear this interaction and ask to speak to him privately. Here's the process for this type of situation:

- Check your own pulse first. Stay calm and know this isn't personal.

- Summarize any past discussions about the behavior in question, if appropriate. Be very brief.

- Acknowledge his emotional state. "I can see that you are upset that the treatment has been delayed."

- State your intention for this discussion. "Although I would like to promise that all delays can be prevented, we both know that is impossible because of unforeseen circumstances. I would like to talk about how we can communicate with you in a calm, professional manner."

- Describe his or her behavior. "You raised your voice to my staff without waiting to hear about the reasons for the delay."

- Describe the impact it is having. "When you do that, it is very disruptive to the entire floor since we can all hear you, and that includes the patients. It stresses everybody."

- State the desired behavior. "In the future, I would appreciate if you would have a calm conversation with my staff or me about whatever looks awry. Once you hear the reasons, I think you'll see that it was out of the nurse's control, which may still

---

EXAMPLE 4 (CONT.)

upset you, but at least you'll know that it was not because someone was shirking his or her duty. Just so that you know, we just had a long code to run that took most of our nursing resources, leaving those who were on the floor to double up on their assignments. When that happens, they have to prioritize the most critical treatments, meds, etc."

- Ask for questions. "Does that make sense? Is there anything else you want to share with me?"

- Offer your appreciation.

Some of you will have the occasion when you have to interact with an "alpha male." These are men who have made it to the top of their profession and have a distinctive interaction style that can be intimidating to others. They tend to have very high opinions of themselves, although they lack self-awareness and awareness of others. Not all men who excel have this type of style; in fact, the best leaders are very collaborative and humanistic. Although women who make it to the top of their profession might be labeled "alpha," women in general tend to be more collaborative and relationship oriented than the "alpha male." "Female leaders are less comfortable with conflict, *while alpha males thrive on it* [emphasis added]. When the alpha male doesn't like something, he states it loud and clear" (Ludeman & Erlandson, 2004). The more intimidated people are by these types, the more they will be avoided, which can result in increased errors. The point is that their behavior, which can be aggressive and domineering and is uncomfortable for others, should not be taken personally. This is easier said than done.

These people need to be confronted or errors will occur. Think back to the 1970s to the worst aviation disaster in history, which occurred on Tenerife Island. The pilot of a

KLM plane decided to take off without tower clearance. The copilot was too intimidated to tell the captain that he was not cleared. The outcome was disastrous. The KLM plane hit a Pan Am plane that was obscured by fog on the runway, killing 583 people.

Most nonalpha people go into "flight" mode and withdraw when an "alpha" is stressed and acting out. Errors happen when people don't speak up. We know that much hospital morbidity and mortality could be prevented if staff were comfortable speaking up. Many hospitals are changing their culture to ensure that this happens.

Preventing problems

Whether you are confronting your staff or your colleagues, you must do it to prevent bigger problems down the road. When confrontation doesn't work, then it's time to escort the person out, either to another position that is better suited for him or her or out of the organization.

As Jim Collins states in *Good to Great*, when you know that you have the wrong person on the bus, act (Collins, 2001). Postponing the decision isn't fair to you, the organization, the employee, or his or her colleagues. They deserve to work at a place that is a good fit for their skills and values.

Even if you aren't completely comfortable with the confrontation process—and not flawlessly skilled at it—doing it is critical and will earn you the respect of your staff and colleagues alike. Rehearse and practice these discussions. Get some feedback from a staff member or colleague. One positive aspect is that most relationships get stronger after these types of discussion. You look strong when you draw a line in the sand, and people need to know where their boundaries are.

References

1. Collins, J. C. (2001). *Good to Great: Why Some Companies Make the Leap—and Others Don't.* New York: HarperCollins Publishers, Inc.

2. Ludeman, K., & Erlandson, E. (2004). "Coaching the alpha male." *Harvard Business Review,* 82(5), 58–67.

3. "Minimizing the risks of discriminatory suits when terminating poor performers." (2001). *Journal of Health-care Management,* 46(2), 134–141.

4. Williams, A. H. (2002). *How to Discipline & Document Employee Behavior.* Brentwood, TN: M. Lee Smith Publishers, LLC.

CHAPTER 11

PERFORMANCE APPRAISALS

Learning Objectives

After reading this chapter, the reader will be able to:

- State the reasons for conducting thorough performance appraisals
- Identify the benefits for incorporating self-appraisals into the process

Since it's pretty universal that everybody hates doing performance appraisals (PAs), why are managers still required to do them? Most managers view the process as tedious, meaningless, and time consuming. Many staff members complain that they are unfair and are a waste of time.

If PAs are done poorly, with little thought or effort, they are a waste of time. However, if the process is done well, with feedback and coaching throughout the year, the process should be meaningful and rather pleasant for both you and your staff. It provides an opportunity for some personal attention, feedback and coaching, and either recognition and/or redirection.

Nobody Likes Doing Performance Appraisals, So Why Bother?

Here are some of the reasons that the PA process is not only important but also necessary to be sure everyone is on the same page. The PA process gives you and your staff the opportunity to review and discuss:

- **Progress toward goals.** Most employees like to know how they are doing and what they need to do to get better. If goals are not being met, you have the opportunity to hear about obstacles and then create solutions so that goals can be met. You have the opportunity to recognize good performance so that it can be sustained, and to recalibrate underperformers and get them back on track.

- **Goals and expectations.** You can offer clarity if needed and check for employees' understanding.

- **Employees' career aspirations.** This is a good time to find out where they want to go with their careers and what you can do to help them. There may be learning opportunities that you are aware of that would suit them very well.

- **Employees' strengths and interests.** Ask what they see as their strengths. Let your staff know what you see as their strengths. Ask them if they have ideas about how you and your team can use their strengths more fully.

- **Skills that employees feel they need to develop.** There may be skill areas that they want to develop, of which you are unaware. This is the perfect time to discuss this area and build a development plan. For example, staff may want to get more comfortable having difficult conversations with colleagues or they may want to develop a skill in order to move to the next level.

- **Problems on the unit.** Get staff observations and ideas of any issues that you should know about but may not. While this is not the time to go into great depth about other issues, it is a good time to let issues surface so that you can schedule a follow-up meeting to discuss them further and brainstorm solutions.

- **Feedback for you.** Ask your staff what you are doing that works well for them and what they would like to see you do differently. If you ask them for feedback, be sure you word it in a way, such as listed previously, that is specific and not general. If you ask them, "How am I doing?" it is quite likely they will say, "Fine" and offer no specifics. Just as they want specifics on their performance, you would also like specifics.

The PA process provides you and your organization with additional benefits. Appraising everyone with the same system allows you to look at your group as a whole and identify any trends and make changes as needed. You might find certain skills or areas where many excel. What are the reasons for that? What is going on that may be significant? Is there a way to leverage that collective strength? Also, are there any areas where many are generally weak? Might you need to look at your hiring practices? What about some additional training?

You might review your unit goals/metrics, and see whether there are any patterns between PA results for a particular area and goals. Does anything jump out at you when you look at your employee satisfaction scores next to your composite PA scores? Assimilating all this data may seem daunting, but taking some time to review it can help you make more accurate plans for your department and use your limited training and development resources more wisely.

For example, you notice that a large percentage of your staff rate low on an item such as "provides feedback to other staff in a constructive manner." This is an indication that some additional training, feedback, and coaching is warranted. However, you should have already been aware of this from your own observation and data collection throughout the year.

Maybe some of your newer staff rated themselves low in confronting colleagues about issues. Since you can't be observing them all the time and since no one has come to you with any specific complaints, you may be unaware of any fear about this topic. Again, this is great information for you to have so you can plan more training, feedback, and coaching in this area. Since many of your newer staff members are probably Generation Yers, know that they are typically very open to learning plans (Lower, 2007). They want to excel and will work hard to achieve the success that they expect.

Reviewing and analyzing your composite data can help you and your colleagues in the human resources (HR) department as you make decisions about promotions, transfers, staffing needs, training needs, and terminations (Chandra, 2006). HR will be reviewing the data from the entire organization to help with its talent plans. It will help you to identify or confirm your top performers, your bottom performers, your emerging leaders, and the needs of your new staff so that you can prescribe precise development. For example, why would you put your entire staff through _____ (you fill in the blank) if this is a deficient area just for your newer staff?

Another benefit of the PA process is that you get to spend some one-on-one time with each member of your team. Employees generally like getting individualized attention from their manager. This helps them feel supported and engaged in their jobs and it helps to build trust between the two of you.

Staff Self-Appraisals

A study by Inderrieden, Allen & Keaveny (2004) indicated that self-ratings have an overall positive effect on the PA process because self-ratings bring another perspective to the appraisal discussion. The fact that people have to think about the appraisal items and flesh out a rationale for their ratings makes the discussion richer. It turns the meeting into a discussion as opposed to a one-way monologue by you. When people have put thought into each item and have input into a discussion, they are much more likely to buy into the process and gain value from it. In most organizations, the days of walking into an appraisal and reading a review are pretty much over. People want to be involved and take ownership of their careers and they want to continue to grow. They want to be engaged; the more input they have into the way things are run, into making decisions that affect them, and into their performance evaluation, the more engaged they are likely to be.

Self-appraisals may not be standard at your organization. If they are not, talk to your manager and HR. The process for employees completing a self-appraisal can include the following steps:

- The employee is sent the appraisal form two to three weeks prior to the appraisal date (which is usually an anniversary date or is the date when the entire organization completes the appraisal process).

- The employee fills out the entire appraisal form. This forces the employee to reflect on his or her performance for the entire year: goals he or she has achieved and specific examples of how he or she has met the expectations for that year. Employees should be encouraged to keep track of goals they have accomplished over the year: projects they have worked on and the degree of success that was achieved from them, certifications, training, new responsibilities, committees, ideas they have implemented, etc. They should be ready to rate themselves on each competency on their appraisal form and have rationale for the rating for each.

- Each staff member should bring his or her completed form to the appraisal discussion that he or she will have with his or her manager.

- The employees should be ready to talk with their manager about goals they would like to achieve for the coming year and how those goals might be accomplished. They should also be ready to talk about their career aspirations and how the manager might help them achieve those goals. They should be prepared to discuss any area where they struggle or feel challenged.

For example, nurses might have some interest in leadership but be unsure whether that route is the best for them. They might find confronting some colleagues' disruptive behavior challenging (other nurses, doctors, etc.) The appraisal discussion is a great time to bring these items to your attention if they have not been discussed previously.

Staff members need to be educated on what *they* can expect to get out of the discussion. They need to know that they should come away with a good understanding of how they are doing, what they should continue doing, and what they need to do differently. If a trusting relationship has been created between the two of you, the employee should feel comfortable discussing any issues that may be hampering his or her level of engagement so that the two of you can dissect the issue to determine the true cause of the disengagement. The employee should also be ready to discuss aspects of the job and the organization that he or she finds most fulfilling. Information on both ends of this spectrum will be very valuable to you so that you can create and implement needed changes. However, if a trusting relationship does not exist, this will be difficult if not impossible.

Steps for Conducting Performance Appraisals

There should *never* be any surprises during a PA discussion, ever, unless you want to degrade trust.

Preparation

You will begin the process by reviewing the entire past year's worth of data that you have gathered. You'll look at all the notes from observations and conversations that you have had with the nurse and others about all performance-related activities, records (critical incidents, attendance, etc.), and any other data points you have access to. You may want to confer with your leadership team or charge nurses to gather any additional data. You will want to complete the appraisal form prior to your discussion with the nurse. During the prep phase, you will want to give a self-evaluation to the nurse so that it can be filled out prior to your meeting as discussed previously. Be sure to give your staff enough time to complete their form.

Planning

This is an important conversation regardless of how well the person has performed. Set up a time and place for a private conversation and do not allow any interruptions during this meeting. You want your staff to take this process seriously, and if the meeting appears to be "on the fly," with interruptions and joking around, the staff member will not appreciate the value and gravitas that the process demands. Be sure to set aside an appropriate amount of time: around 45 minutes, even if the person is a star performer.

Although typically the problem performers take most of your time and attention, in reality your best performers should get the lion's share of your time and attention. They have earned your attention and you want them to feel supported in their continued positive trajectory. They will also have great ideas to share with you about ways to make the team stronger and how to shore up any deficient areas. Pay attention to your stars.

Identify specific accomplishments for which you want to offer appreciation and congratulations and recognition. Likewise, note any areas where additional coaching is needed or plans need to be made for goal accomplishment.

The appraisal form may contain some or all of the following categories: clinical expertise, protocol, professional relationships, professional commitment/involvement, professional development, attendance/availability, etc. (Meilman, 2001). The form you use may include different headers, but regardless, the process is the same.

Sharing information

This is the appraisal discussion; it really is an exchange of information.

Open by letting the staff member know the process for the review:

1. You will review each item one by one.

2. The staff member will share his or her rating and rationale first.

3. You will then share your rating and rationale.

4. Together, you will come to agreement on the rating. Your rating should be
    very close if not identical since you have been coaching the employee since
    your last appraisal discussion. If you rated the person higher on an item,
    that rating should stand without much disagreement from the nurse. If the
    employee's is higher than yours, be ready to provide rationale for your rat-
    ing. If he or she has data of which you were unaware, don't be afraid to
    change your rating to the higher value. That shows you are open to input.
    This is not a negotiation, however, and compromise is not an appropriate
    method for resolving differences. You want to arrive at the most accurate
    assessment.

5. Discuss plans to develop any skills that need development (which does not
    necessarily mean deficiency) or goals that need to be attained and that were
    not realized during the previous evaluation period.

6. Discuss any new goals and steps for achievement.

7. Review career aspirations and plans to get to the next step.

8. Review strengths, interests, and plans to leverage them.

9. Ask if there is anything else he or she wants to share or any ideas he or she has.

10. Summarize strengths, accomplishments, efforts, and plans for the coming
    year.

Express appreciation and close the meeting

Always close the meeting by reminding staff that you are there to help them be the best they can be and that you are always happy to talk with them about their ideas and suggestions for improvement of the department or if they are experiencing any difficulties. Ask for feedback on you (what they like and would like to see more of and what they would like to see you do differently).

Postmeeting

Note any development planning actions that you need to take and when you need to follow up with staff again.

Rating errors

Since there are no perfect managers, a discussion of common rating errors follows. These are typical traps that anyone can slip into without conscious effort. Here's a list of the most common errors:

- **Varying standards.** The same standards need to be applied evenly to everyone in the same job class.

- **Recency effect.** This error occurs when you give heavier weight to recent performance rather than evaluating performance over the entire period. This error is very common and raters need to be conscious of the tendency to apply recency.

- **Rater bias** (gender, age, experience, race, ethnicity). Biases of the raters may be subconscious and unintended. But you must not rate your staff differently because of your preference toward any particular demographic.

- **Halo and horn effect.** This effect occurs when the entire evaluation is shadowed by someone's stellar performance in one area (e.g., clinical expertise) or his or her poor performance in one area (e.g., documentation).

- **Contrast error.** This error occurs when everyone is rated against the performance of others versus against standards. For example, if everyone performs very well in one area, and someone is not quite as good, you shouldn't rate that person low. Rate performance against standards, not "everyone else."

- **Central tendency, leniency, and strictness errors.** When a rater scores everyone down the middle (central tendency) so that they don't have to have any difficult discussions or because they are not diligent, the PA process is rendered useless. Likewise, if a rater rates everyone very harshly (strictness error) or rates everyone very highly (and it is unwarranted), again the process becomes meaningless.

If you don't do appraisals routinely—routinely meaning you do everybody's appraisal at the same time of year (instead of according to their hire dates)—review these errors before beginning the process just to remind yourself about them. It could make the difference between having a great and rewarding discussion with your staff and having the conversation be a waste of time.

Manager Training

One of the reasons that managers and employees dislike the PA process, as mentioned previously, is because oftentimes managers are untrained in a thorough process and in how to conduct such a meeting. It takes some training and practice to get good. It's just like interviewing. You need training to understand the principles and practice to apply the skills and smooth out your rough edges.

Think about a nurse with no surgical experience and minimal surgical training who was asked to scrub in on a procedure. Instead of being a resource to the surgical team, she merely put the instruments on the mayo stand and said to the team, "Here. Just take what you need." (This actually happened.)

It's the same thing that used to occur with PAs. The manager would write it and give it to the employee to read. No interaction, no help, no coaching, no goal setting. No wonder people found the process unfulfilling.

If you have never received any training in how to hold this valuable discussion with your staff, put it on your development plan to get some training. There may be several managers in your organization who need the training as well. Or perhaps there is an experienced manager who can work with you one-on-one to build your skills to make this process valuable to both you and your staff.

References

1. Chandra, A. (2006). "Employee evaluation strategies for healthcare organizations – A general guide." *Hospital Topics: Research and Perspectives on Healthcare*, 84(2), 34–38.

2. Inderrieden, E. J., Allen, R. E., & Keaveny, T. J. (2004). "Managerial discretion in the use of self-ratings in an appraisal system: The antecedents and consequences." *Journal of Managerial Issues*, 16(4), 460–482.

3. Lower, J. (2007). "Brace yourself here comes Generation Y." *American Nurse Today*, 2(8), 26–29.

4. Meilman, Philip W. (2001). "Human resource issues in university health services." *Journal of American College Health,* 50, 43–48.

5. Smith, M. H. (2003). "Empower staff with praiseworthy appraisals." *Nursing Management,* 34(1), 16-17.

CHAPTER 12

COACHING AND MENTORING THROUGH CHANGE

Learning Objectives

After reading this chapter, the reader will be able to:

- Explain why nurses need to be adaptable

- List barriers to change

Change can be unpredictable. Nursing leaders need to be on top of the shifting forces that create the need for a rapid response, and they need to communicate these changes to their staff and help them make sense of the apparent confusion. Staff nurses need coaching to help them make the leap from entrenched patterns to new practices.

The external environment is shifting at a breakneck rate—remember how the external environment affects an organization and its culture? The way that medicine and nursing are being practiced has changed and will continue to change. As a leader, take note of all these changes. Communicate them to your staff members so that they get a sense that change is on its way. Agility is a requirement for survival today.

Why Do People Resist Change?

Humans are hardwired to resist change as long as the status quo is secure and comfortable. And the longer a practice has been in place, the more entrenched it is and the harder it is to change it. Vermeulen, Puranam, and Gulati (2010) refer to this as "the accretion of deadening routines." However, when someone feels threatened or that the status quo is no longer acceptable or possible, change becomes much more amenable.

If your hospital has not moved to an electronic medical record (EMR) system, think about how challenging this change will be. Nurses have been writing on paper charts since the beginning of the practice a couple hundred years ago. Talk about an entrenched practice! If not there already, EMR is coming to your hospital—and planning for its successful implementation is your job. Your coaching and communication skills need to be in shape to help staff traverse the abyss with as little collateral damage as possible.

> *"If you do not change, you can become extinct."*
> —*Johnson (1998)*

When change becomes inevitable, sometimes people go into shock and denial. They may not be prepared for the change of life that is upon them and choose not to deal with it at the time. Later, they may feel angry: "It's not fair. Why don't *they* fix it? We just changed 'X' process." This anger can lead to resentment and disenfranchisement. Morale can drop. People may try to redirect the proposed change so that it doesn't affect them, but rather someone else. They may attempt to soften the magnitude of the change. They may become passive-defensive or aggressive-defensive. Eventually, they realize that the change is not going away and that they need to either get on board or leave. They accept reality.

Sound familiar? The process just described is Kübler-Ross' stages of grief, which can be extrapolated to the feelings associated with the change process. The reason that this works is that the primary reason people resist change is because of their fear of loss. With fear comes the general adaptation syndrome: fight or flight.

Resistance to change derails some of the best change processes. Too often, managers meet resistance with force, which is a common reaction but rarely constructive. With change, as with most things, sheer force doesn't work. Rather than pushing their agenda on others, change agents should seek to engage resisters and learn more about what is behind the opposition. They should view it as feedback, not defiance (Ford & Ford, 2009). Instead of quelling the resistance, embrace and get into it. Find out what is behind it and where the fears are coming from. Often the fears are unfounded, but if they remain unarticulated, you will never know and thus not have the opportunity to share the correct information. Often, the resisters will have ideas that can add to the quality of the change process.

LEADERSHIP TIP

Expect and plan for resistance; do not be afraid of it.

Anxiety comes from fear of not knowing how to use a new product or process, so training and support should always accompany any large departure from the routine. There may be people who, even after attempts to include their ideas and feedback, still do not "get with the program." For those who still don't want to comply, separation may be inevitable. Fortunately, in most cases, this is rare.

The Change Process

The change process, which John Kotter (1996) brilliantly describes in eight steps, can be boiled down into three distinct phases: preparation, implementation, and postimplementation.

Preparation

Change efforts fail usually not because of unneeded changes or poorly thought out changes, but because of a lack of due diligence during preliminary planning. The first phase, therefore, of any change process is the preparation phase. At this point, it has become apparent that some type of change is necessary to respond to the pressures of the environment. These *pressures* might be for better communication among colleagues, a new process to satisfy customers, products or services to match or outpace the competition, meeting Joint Commission standards, increasing employee satisfaction, etc. Pressure necessitates some kind of change.

The need for change has been established, but it is common that people will resist change. The following are the questions you should consider prior to making a change:

- How entrenched is the current practice? The thicker the "rope" or routine, the harder it will be to break, and the more planning it will require to thaw the status quo.

- How prepared are the team members for this imminent change? In other words, have you, their manager, been communicating to them about the environmental pressures being exerted on them or the organization? Or will this blindside them? The less prepped they are, the more up-front work that will need to take place.

- How used to change are they? The more your staff is used to change, the easier it will be.

If your team members are low on the change-readiness continuum, there will be a longer lead time to prepare them. Some activities that will need to be completed prior to implementation to help improve readiness are:

- Establish a group to lead the change on your unit. Kotter (1996) calls this the "guiding coalition." This group will lead the change on your unit. The group may be just a few people, depending on the magnitude of the project, but it should include staff with credibility, leadership skills, and informal influence abilities.

- Create a communication plan. The more ingrained the practice and the more staff are emotionally bound to the practice, the bigger the need for abundant communication. This should come from you, the manager, as well as the guiding team. Identify "what's in it for me" (WIIFM). Let staff know how this will help them and communicate this frequently. They need to know how this will, in the end, make their lives better. Your communication plan should include who you will communicate to, the vehicle (group meeting, personal meeting, e-mail, poster, etc.), timing (dates), and the responsible party (who is in charge of the communication).

- Address resistance. Not everyone will overtly express resistance. Watch body language. Keep your ears open. Invite staff to talk to you about it. Talk with them privately if needed since some may not want to verbalize their fears or concerns in front of others. Listen to the feelings behind the content. Coach your guiding team on how to listen to concerns and get input. Your staff may have some great ideas on how to make the change easier or more effective.

- Get staff input into how the change will transpire. The more input you get into any change, the more buy-in you are likely to have.

- Create and communicate the vision (Kotter, 1996). Paint the picture of what the future will look like. Make it appealing to your staff. The change team should create the vision and be ready to articulate it.

- Provide skills training and the time and opportunity to practice. This is a crucial step if the change requires new skills. Be sure the training is thorough and that practice time is adequate.

Sometimes changes come down from above and there is little that anyone can do about them. An example is a change to the organization's benefits plan. Although this is an area that all employees hold dear, since it affects their pocketbooks, all departments are under financial pressures and sometimes employees have little recourse if their overall benefits are decreased. Although no one is happy about a reduction in benefits, it might be more understandable if the team had been kept aware of the institution's overall financial situation. Again, communication about trends and pressures is key.

Implementation

Kick off the implementation with some hoopla. You and the guiding team need to express and share enthusiasm for the process of crossing the abyss to the new way of doing things. The change team should keep the vision front and center and communicate it frequently.

You should go first. You *must* walk the talk with passion. What you do and how you do it is much more important than what you say. If the change is something large, like an EMR system or an electronic pharmacy delivery system, be a role model and use it on day one. It's okay if you have to struggle with it at first, look at your notes, or have an "expert" help you. This will show the rest of the team that it's okay if you don't get it perfectly the first time. It will allay their fears and make them more comfortable with the new product or process.

Provide support and encouragement during this stage. When people are struggling with something new, they experience less anxiety if someone is nearby to support and encourage them. Always have support assembled ahead of time, which might be you or a member of the guiding team. When possible, have this person on the unit until everyone is comfortable. An "800" tech support number doesn't hurt, but is nowhere near as effective as having a person there to help your staff cross the abyss.

Ask for feedback on how the new process is working out. Find out what is working and what isn't. Determine whether there are any glitches and fix them quickly. Continue getting feedback to determine comfort and skill level.

During the change, celebrate small wins. As people get used to the new system or product, have them share their successes with the other staff. Ask them to share their insights on what went well, what they did differently, and what the outcome was. Recognize and celebrate the successes quickly. Success might eventually look like increased safety, reduced errors, reduced time, increased employee satisfaction, or increased customer satisfaction. Track these results as you get them and share with the staff.

Postimplementation

Plan to hold debriefing meetings with your guiding team to discuss what went well, what didn't, and the lessons learned. Record this and share it with the team. Ask the staff the same questions: What went well, what didn't, and what should have been done differently? If there were implementation issues, try to get an idea from your team and staff as to how pervasive they were. Be sure to celebrate all the things that went well.

You want to anchor the new practice into the culture (Kotter, 1996). There may be some practices that were firmly entrenched in the old way of doing things that are not part of the new culture. You need to recognize when artifacts of the old way need to end. Don't take this lightly. It is disconcerting when an entrenched way of life has to end. It's like when someone discovers he or she has very high cholesterol levels and must stop his or her routine of eating a big bowl of ice cream every evening or a daily bacon and egg breakfast.

There was a labor and delivery unit that used a large wipe-off board that displayed patients' OB details. All patients were listed with details about their gravity and parity, and current health issues including STDs, fetal condition, substance abuse, etc. It was in the middle of the unit, clearly visible for anyone to see. You can imagine the privacy issues, so it had to go when they moved to an electronic charting system that incorporated fetal monitoring. Staff would now be able to view all this information electronically and confidentially. It was a substantial implementation process that required new skills and new behaviors.

The problem was that the "board" was where change of shift report took place for all clinical staff: nurses, physicians, residents, and students. It was an artifact of the culture. Everyone congregated around the board not only at report time, but also at any time that the stress level was building. It was a communication tool and a decision-making tool. It bound the staff together. It was a deeply entrenched part of the daily routine.

Simply removing the board when the time came would have been disconcerting to the team members. Of course, they would have adapted quickly, but it made much more sense to make a big deal about the "death" of such an integral artifact. Therefore, the team announced the date of the demise of the board so that people could prepare themselves. As the removal date arrived, there was a brief "ceremony" when the last patient's name was wiped off the board, each team member signed the board, and it was removed. It now resides on the wall of a break room, a fond reminder of days gone by. Eventually, it will become meaningless. However, while people still work there who remember the "old days," it provides a piece of nostalgia, an artifact of the old culture.

When preparing for change, think about ways to fasten the new process onto the culture. Talk about the new norms of behavior. Link the new way of doing things to better outcomes for patients and staff. Make this information overt and communicate it frequently. Celebrate when new goals are met or when there is incremental movement toward them.

LEADERSHIP TIP

Barriers to change include:

- **Lack of input from those who will be affected by the change.** When staff members are not asked for their input, crossing the abyss will be challenging. The more they can be engaged early on, the less likely they are to resist. It will give them a sense of being in control of the process rather than being a victim of it.

- **Lack of communication.** As a manager, you are kept up to date by senior management on current issues in your organization, community, and the broader healthcare industry. Share this information with your staff members so that they too keep up to date with trends that may ultimately affect them.

- **Structures and processes.** Structures and processes that get in the way of a change effort include the organizational chart, hierarchy, or reporting structure. Even physical structures such as walls may need to come down for better communication or patient visibility, or one may need to go up so that there is more patient privacy. Processes that can either support or thwart a change effort include compensation, time recording, scheduling, communication, and leadership development. Be sure the structures and processes are aligned with the change you are trying to effect. Get rid of the ones that get in your way.

Coaching and Mentoring Through a Change Process

Remember that for most people, changing behavior is stressful because it evokes fear of loss. Your staff members need feedback, coaching, and mentoring through the change process to help them feel supported in crossing the abyss. Help them be leaders, who are in front of the change not behind it. Leadership and innovation go hand in hand. Leaders look to the future and learn from the past (Kouzes & Posner, 2002). Help staff to always challenge the status quo and look for better ways to do things. Role model for them, and support and guide them to ask the right questions. Catch them acting like leaders and give lots of positive feedback. Be a mentor when they feel like they are losing their way. Get them back on the right path.

"People underestimate their capacity for change. There is never a right time to do a difficult thing. A leader's job is to help people have vision of their potential."
—*John Porter*

In summary, here is how you can make change easier:

- Seek staff member's ideas early. Go to them with the problem and let them come up with a better way. They will be much more on board if they have input. "A change imposed is a change opposed" (Johnson, 1998).

- Communicate, communicate, communicate.

- Help staff cross the abyss. Lead the way. You should go first.

- Give staff the support they need to try the new process in a safe environment (training and coaching).

- Help staff visualize the new way of doing things as being better. Help them paint the picture.

- Trust the new way and help staff see that they too can trust it.

- Celebrate little wins.

- Get their input on how to dispense with the old behaviors and artifacts, and embed the new in the culture.

"When you're finished changing, you're finished."
— *Benjamin Franklin*

References

1. Ford, J. D., & Ford, L. W. (2009). "Decoding resistance to change." *Harvard Business Review*, 87(4), 99–103.

2. Johnson, S. (1998). *Who Moved My Cheese?* New York: G. P. Putnam's Sons Publishers.

3. Kotter, J. P. (1996). *Leading Change.* Boston: Harvard Business School Press.

4. Kouzes, J. M., & Posner, B. Z. (2002). *The Leadership Challenge* (3rd ed.). San Francisco: Jossey-Bass.

5. Vermeulen, F., Puranam, P., & Gulati, R. (2010). "Change for change's sake." *Harvard Business Review*, 88(6), 70–76.

CHAPTER 13

CELEBRATING SUCCESS

Learning Objectives

After reading this chapter, the reader will be able to:

- Explain the importance of celebrating success

- Describe how to make celebrations meaningful

"The magic of special occasions is vital in building significance into collective life."
—*Bolman and Deal (1995)*

Everyone wants to feel significant and that their lives and their work matter. Symbolic expressions such as celebrations help to make people feel significant by publicly marking an achievement or transition. Self-esteem needs get met when people feel significant.

Think back to the last celebration you attended: wedding, baptism, funeral, birthday, going-away party, promotion, graduation, bar mitzvah, retirement, housewarming, baby, etc. Who was the honoree and what did they do? What was the event like? Describe the elements that made it a "celebration." Who else was there? Why did you attend? How did you feel? Chances are you attended the event because you are a friend or relative of the honoree and you wanted to pay tribute to the person and recognize the *transition* or *achievement* that was being celebrated. You probably attended to support that person and to share and enhance what they were feeling.

Why Celebration Is Important

The purpose of celebration is to mark the significance of an event and to bring people together to share in the emotion of the occasion, thereby allowing everyone in attendance to *feel more*. In our high-tech world, where life is becoming more virtual every day and interaction with other humans continues to diminish, our personal bonds suffer. We have tight bonds with fewer people. In general, we feel less.

Celebrations remind us to connect emotionally with those whose accomplishments or transitions are being honored and with the others at the event whom we may not even know well. They help us to pause, recognize, offer words of support, and *share* the feeling of joy.

Your organization, department, or unit is no different. Leaders need to commit to celebrations to recognize individual and collective achievement to bring everyone together, build team cohesion, and ignite the spirit that build bonds of collectivity and belonging.

Culture

Celebrations are part of the symbolic framework of your organization and help to embed behaviors, thoughts, beliefs, and values into your organization's culture. Look back at the map of organizational culture in Chapter 2 (Figure 2.1). Note that celebrations appear at the top of the map along with the other symbolic expressions of the culture. Celebrations, therefore, become a way to reinforce and encourage specific behaviors.

> *"Celebrate what you want to see more of."*
> —Thomas J. Peters

Symbols to use during your celebrations can include things like pins, plaques, certificates, etc. It is more important to have symbols than to have expensive symbols.

> ## LEADERSHIP TIP
>
> Without celebration, life is drudgery: a series of forgettable days, years, decades, lives.

Meaning

"The gift of significance lets people find meaning in work, faith in themselves, confidence in the value of their lives, and hope for the future. Reason and technology often divert our attention from the everyday existential pillars that support our sense of significance" (Bolman & Deal, 1995).

Values

People pay attention to what their leader pays attention to, so give careful thought to the results and accomplishments that you decide to recognize and celebrate. Your celebrations and recognitions should flow from the values of your organization, your department, and your unit. As you think about what you want to celebrate and recognize, start with your values.

Why Recognition Is Important

Recognition is typically one of the most cited reasons that people work, yet is also something that most don't receive. People want meaningful, important work that is noticed by others. Recognition from managers is very important to employees regardless of industry; recognition makes employees feel important. The connotation of acknowledgment from supervisors is caring and support. Remember Maslow? Self-esteem is a universal human need. When managers recognize the accomplishments or transitions of their staff, they are helping to get that need met. People who have their needs met are happy, productive, take risks, use their strengths, and intend to stay with the organization (AbuAlRub & Al-Zaru, 2008). Recognition energizes and motivates the honoree, can inspire and motivate others as well, and gives a tremendous amount of satisfaction to the manager. Everybody wins. (See Figure 13.1.)

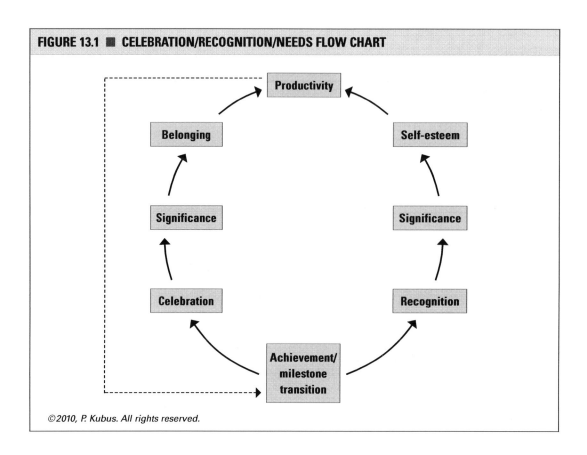

FIGURE 13.1 ■ CELEBRATION/RECOGNITION/NEEDS FLOW CHART

How to Celebrate and Recognize

Consider recruiting a nurse on your unit to help you manage this program. It is a great developmental activity for someone you are grooming for management. You need a champion to take the helm. Do not turn a group loose on this project without your guidance up front. You will need to give them background and rationale on the purpose of the program and the objectives. They, in turn, can elicit help from a group of staff to craft the recognition and celebration program. Empower them whenever you can. Getting ideas from staff about how best to recognize their teammates and celebrate their accomplishments will make the program more meaningful to them. And that's what this is all about.

The following describes the process for your "Celebration Project Team" and you:

- Create a Celebration Project Team consisting of one of your leadership nurses or charge nurses, and one nurse from each level (Level IV, III, II, etc.) and each shift (if possible). They should have fun with this project and put some voltage behind it.

- Review the mission and vision statements.

- Review the values of the organization, department, and/or unit.

- Determine the budget for this project. If you have absolutely nothing to spend, have part of the project team's charter be to find some funding or come up with creative ways to celebrate for free. If you find vendors for monthly celebrations, figure out how much it would cost to sponsor your celebration and invite vendors to attend. This does not have to require a lot of money.

- Determine professional manifestations (the "what") of the mission, vision, and values for:

  - The team: goal achievement (patient satisfaction scores, reduction in overtime, employee satisfaction scores, etc.)

  - Individuals: promotions, new hires, new certifications, training completion, new degrees, project completion or milestone, organization anniversaries, transfers, retirements, accomplishments, etc.

  - Determine whether you want to acknowledge personal transitions: birthdays, new house, new baby, marriage; consider including birthdays since everyone has one, therefore everyone will be included at some point during the year

The Celebration Project Team can determine the following and then present their recommendations to you:

- The "how." Determine who will make the presentations and how they will be done (certificates, etc.). One idea is to have one of the project team members emcee the celebration and you, the manager, hand out the award and make comments. Someone should take pictures of the event for possible use at other events. An annual DVD that has all the awards and recipients would be great to give out at the end of the year to each staff member. Invite your service director, chief nursing officer, and CEO; the more brass, the better. Let them hand out the awards or at least be in front with you to shake each person's hand and thank him or her personally. Ask them to share a few comments at the end.

- The magnitude and frequency of the celebration:
  - Monthly, quarterly, annually
  - Location: on the unit or at an outside location (e.g., for a holiday party) or some of each
  - Timing: one celebration per shift, preferably at the beginning; you should attend each

- The outcome. You and your Celebration Project Team should do a quick debriefing after each event. Think about what went well and what you might want to change for next time.

"Enthusiasm is one of the most powerful engines of success. When you do a thing, do it with your might. Put your whole soul into it. Stamp it with your own personality. Be active, be energetic, be enthusiastic and faithful, and you will accomplish your objective. Nothing great was ever achieved without enthusiasm."
—*Ralph Waldo Emerson*

Recognition options

There are many books available that offer ideas about how to recognize staff in ways that are meaningful but inexpensive. You can find lots of ideas on the Internet. Listed here are some ideas of simple and inexpensive ways to acknowledge the accomplishments and transitions of your staff:

- Make a big deal to welcome and recognize new staff. Let everyone know when new people will be starting and share new staff's background. Be there on their first day to personally welcome them and introduce them to the rest of the team. Help everyone feel significant. Be sure that one of your expectations is that all staff members welcome new staff and offer their help and support.

  - Think about the manager who does not let the staff know in advance about a newcomer who is about to join the team. The new person just shows up and no one knows anything about this person's background. How important does your staff feel? How does the new person feel?

- A handwritten note of recognition or thanks or congratulations shows people you care. It makes them feel significant. Keep a copy of your note in the employee's file. Make it timely. Write the note as soon as possible after the event.

- Share accomplishments verbally with the rest of the staff at a staff meeting or celebration, whichever is appropriate. Public recognition is almost always a motivator for most people (but not for everyone).

- Spend time with the person; give feedback and coaching, mentor, get his or her ideas for the future, take the honoree to lunch (birthdays perhaps). People want to spend time with you; it makes them feel special.

- Provide learning and exposure opportunities. Recognize staff members by sending them to a workshop and having them report back on what they learned. Have employee attend a managers' meeting with you or represent you at the meeting.

CASE STUDY

One manager tells the following story:

My team has had such a busy few years. We've grown a lot and everyone has worked really hard. Recognition wasn't at the top of my priority list. However, just last week we had a meeting of the entire staff, and some awards were given out to people who had really gone above and beyond. We didn't have any quantitative metrics to assess, so our awards were all subjective. I asked the CEO to come to the meeting to give out the wards, which were just certificates of excellence and appreciation. That's all.

I had no idea that this would be such a success. After the awards ceremony, the atmosphere in the room was electric. Those who had been recognized were congratulated by everyone else in the room. They said things like: "This is the first time I've ever been recognized! It was the coolest thing." "I loved being recognized in front of my peers and the CEO!" "What I do really does bring value to the organization!"

The importance of recognizing achievements and taking time to celebrate them cannot be overstated. Doing so builds self-esteem and helps create a sense of belonging to a group. In the long run, celebrations and recognition not only help your staff feel significant but also increase productivity and a build sense of cohesion. It takes some time and a little bit of money to build a program that works for you, but the personal and professional payoff for you and your staff is enormous.

References

1. AbuAlRub, R. F., & Al-Zaru, I. M. (2008). "Job stress, recognition, job performance and intention to stay at work among Jordanian hospital nurses." *Journal of Nursing Management*, 16(3), 227–236.

2. Bolman, L. G., & Deal, T. E. (1995). *Leading with Soul*. San Francisco: Jossey-Bass.

3. Deal, T. E., & Key, M. K. (1998). *Corporate Celebration: Play, Purpose, and Profit at Work*. San Francisco: Berrett-Koehler.

4. Whyte, L. (2008). "Celebrating success." *Nursing Management*, 15(6), 10–11.

CHAPTER 14

DEVELOPING FUTURE NURSING LEADERS

Learning Objectives

After reading this chapter, the reader will be able to:

- Describe the goals of a good leadership development program

- Explain the benefits of mentoring

So many hospitals today go outside the organization to find the best leaders for all levels; in fact, some hospitals hire most of their executive-level leaders from the outside. Hiring from the outside has the benefit of bringing in new ideas, new ways of doing things, different perspectives, and a proven record of accomplishment. However, if done routinely, it can lead to disenfranchisement and turnover of good employees. Good future leaders will go elsewhere to get the development they need to reach their own potential. Developing future leaders is part of a sound retention strategy.

Developing Future Leaders (or Building Your Leadership Bench Strength)

Who will replace you and your peers when you move on? This used to be a question in nursing that was infrequently considered until it was urgent. All too often, in nursing, medicine, and pharmacy, a clinical expert is put into a leadership position and then gets some leadership development. Leadership and management skills are very different from technical skills. When someone enters a new role for which he or she is not

© 2010 HCPro, Inc.

prepared, the learning curve is steep and rocky. The person struggles with the new challenges with which he or she is suddenly faced, frustration and stress build, staff morale drops, turnover increases, and patient care suffers. Taking steps to thwart that painful sequence of events takes some time, effort, and resources, but the payoff in having people ready and willing to lead pays huge dividends in the future, both financially and emotionally.

Most nurses don't go into nursing to become managers. However, along the way and for various reasons, clinicians become interested in management. This can happen when a staff nurse finds him- or herself being managed by a great nurse manager who is an inspirational role model. Others think about management as a means to satisfy their intellectual curiosity and affect more people (Eiser, 2008). Some never consider it until approached by someone who recognizes their potential.

> *"A lot of people have gone further than they thought they could because someone else thought they could."*
> —*Unknown author*

Nursing has made great strides to identify leadership potential and to nurture and develop it, but continued work needs to be done to make the process more efficient and effective. Developing a succession planning process that is intertwined with a sound leadership development program can create a sound roster of potential leaders who are ready to lead when the need arises (Conger & Fulmer, 2003).

Identifying Potential

In many hospitals, especially with physicians, admission to leadership development programs is by application (McAlearney et al. 2005). While these types of situations typically include selection criteria (stated objectives for the program and previous leadership experiences, etc.), it makes more economic sense for participation to be by invitation only (as opposed to application). The benefit of this course of action is that only those who have demonstrated leadership abilities or potential as determined by you and your manager gain access to the program. A good leadership development program can run thousands of dollars per participant per year, so resources should be used wisely on those who appear to have the interest and potential to excel at leadership.

There are many ways to develop a list of invitees. A common practice is for managers, their managers, and the talent development human resources (HR) representative to get together and determine the criteria that must be met for someone to be designated as "high potential." Some criteria on which the person can be evaluated in his or her current role include:

- Experience, years of service

- Education

- Committee service

- Professional association activity

- Trait/competency manifestation (including commitment to mission, vision, and values; ability to build trust; interpersonal skills; adaptability; technical expertise; clinical expertise; foresight; initiative; team playing; risk taking; innovation)

- Leadership experience (including charge nurse role, project leadership)

Your group can determine minimum thresholds for each of the criteria listed above. If your group is looking at this from a service level, nurse managers should not feel they must have someone from their unit to nominate if they truly don't have anybody who is ready. Only the best people should be invited to enter into the development process. As others become ready, they can be evaluated and nominated. This process should be viewed from the service level, and all managers will be involved with helping to develop this group since everyone will benefit and anyone in the group could someday become your peer.

You should have already identified competencies for the leadership role. In addition to those listed previously, additional competencies could include managing change, inspiring and living the vision, commitment to personal and professional growth, communication, building relationships across functional areas, influencing others, decision-making, financial acumen, and strategic planning.

Your staff members have probably not had the opportunity to demonstrate skill or knowledge in all of the leadership competencies, so you have to think about whether, with some instruction and mentoring, they will be able to excel in these areas if they should become a leader. If they are accepted into the group of "high potentials," you can always ask them where they feel their strengths and weaknesses are in those areas so that development can be tailored to their individual needs. As you put their development program together, remember not to focus only on weaknesses. You always want to help them to continue to build on their strengths.

Once you have identified those who have leadership potential, ask each person if he or she is interested in joining this group. Let them know what is involved in terms of the time and effort that will be expected and the goals of the process. They also need to know that they can opt out at any time if they feel this is not what they want to do or they cannot meet the requirements. Opting out does not preclude them from future acceptance; they can always reenter at a later date. Acceptance into this program does not entitle them to promotions; they need to know this at the outset also. The program helps to build future leaders but it makes no promises of promotion. All of the program expectations need to be communicated clearly at the start.

Leadership Development Programs

If you don't have a leadership development process in place for "high potentials," work on this with your talent development HR person, who has expertise in this area. If lack of resources prohibits a formal high potential nursing leadership development program, there are several activities that you can conduct on your unit. You can start to assess and develop talent by asking your staff whether they are interested in leadership and whether they would like to participate in committees projects, and/or become preceptors, charge nurses, etc. There are many activities they can do that cost nothing and can be great learning experiences for them. See also the sections later in this chapter on delegation and action learning projects. Be sure to provide staff with support, coaching, and mentoring if they are new to any of the activities listed.

Even without a formal hospital-endorsed program, you can begin to develop your future charge nurses and assistant nurse managers. This kind of development will make the transition to the new roles much more comfortable for them and will shorten their ramp-up time.

Goals

The goal of a leadership development program is to create depth in leadership bench strength so that leaders are ready to move into new roles as soon as the situation presents itself, thereby reducing role vacancy time and ramp up time. The way to do that is to develop a program to:

- Build self-awareness
  - Identify strengths and weaknesses
  - Conduct personality assessments
- Build organizational and industry understanding
  - Increase visibility to others in the organization
  - Build working relationships with others outside of one's work unit
  - Build awareness of organizational and industry issues
- Build new skills through learning and application
- Build leadership confidence

Training

Development of skills almost always includes some formal training sessions. The benefits of classroom training are that you can be confident that your potential leaders are being exposed to the type of content that you have determined to be important, and that they are all being exposed to the same content. For the foundational information that is deemed critical and to ensure that everyone is on the same page, develop training programs that match the needs of the group.

Typical training programs for new or potential leaders are focused in the areas of communication, building trust, coaching and delegation, managing performance appraisal systems and discussions, project management, interviewing and hiring, progressive discipline, financial acumen, and managing change. These are the foundational skills for any new leader, but your organization may have a slightly different list.

Your training programs must have a component included that allows learners to practice the new skill. Think about when you learned to drive a car. You probably had some classroom instruction where you learned the rules of the road, and the important reasons you do what you do while driving, like maintaining a safe distance from other cars. All the instructions are great, but how different was it when you actually got behind the wheel for the first time? An "A" on the test doesn't ensure that you will be a safe, confident driver. That's why driver education always includes driving a car. The same is true for your training programs; they must include skill practice.

What if you had instruction but didn't get behind the wheel until a year later? How confident would you feel that you could get from here to there safely? While driving with a permit, you must have another licensed driver with you in the car. This is designed to help build confidence and keep you safe. The next element of a good training program must include transfer of training back to the workplace. This is where you come in. After any of your people have been to a training program, sit down and talk to them about it and be sure you afford them the opportunity to apply the knowledge in the workplace. If they just learned interviewing, be sure they get to practice interviewing within a few weeks of the instruction. If you don't have anybody to interview at the time, find someone who does. Your HR department is always interviewing candidates. Ask your HR representative if your nurse can sit in on and participate in one of the interviews that HR is doing.

L E A D E R S H I P   T I P

Training will be wasted (in terms of both time and money) if there isn't application shortly after the program.

Delegation

Delegating projects to high-potential leaders is a great way to help them develop their skills. Since you will know what their strengths and weaknesses are, think about any tasks or projects where they will be able to apply what they know and develop some additional skills. Set learning goals for any delegated work so that they are aware of the skill they are building.

Delegation is a great developmental option as long as the person is supported during the process. Merely dropping a task or project in the person's lap without expectations and guidance and support from you will lead to frustration (although a little is okay and can help the learning process) and failure. Be sure to let the person know that you are always available to review his or her progress and answer his or her questions. There is a fine line between too much guidance, which will remove much of the learning, and too little, which will build frustration (Hudson, 2008). Be very clear with the parameters of the project and your expectations. Let the rest of your staff know that this person is in charge of this project, if appropriate.

The types of projects or tasks that can be delegated can involve improved quality or safety projects, staffing, communication, practice changes, etc. When considering what to delegate and what to do yourself, think about the impact of someone else doing this instead of you. Sometimes you need to be the one seen at the helm of an initiative, but that doesn't mean that you have to do all the tasks yourself. Be sure that what you delegate has learning value. And, of course, you can never delegate any confidential human resource issues.

Delegated projects and tasks provide a great opportunity for feedback and coaching. Check in with the person as he or she is working on a project to see how he or she is doing and review his or her work if needed. Give feedback on his or her work thus far. Coach him or her on how to handle situations that he or she is not clear about or on situations that he or she might have done differently. Ask what questions he or she has and what he or she is learning. Give support and celebrate his or her success. Help to build his or her confidence. Many star performers lack confidence (Berglas, 2006). Give sincere and personal praise for a job well done and for stretching him- or herself and taking a risk.

Action learning

Action learning is one of the best ways to learn new skills. Action learning is the process of having a small group of learners address an actual problem as opposed to a hypothetical problem such as a case study. Case studies are a great tool to use during training programs, but action-learning projects are highly effective because they involve the application of problem-solving skills in real time on a real problem.

The goal is for the group members to identify a real problem, have them work together toward its resolution, create a solution, implement the solution, and then evaluate the results in a quantifiable manner. The last step in an action-learning project is to present the results to management.

The group who will take on an action-learning project can all be from one department, from several departments, or from cross-functional departments. An example of an action-learning project that might require group composition from cross-functional areas is an investigation into medication errors. The group might consist of nurses from one or more services, representatives from pharmacy, and possibly someone from information technology (IT).

Some examples of action-learning projects are reduction of pharmacy errors, reduction in the number of falls, improvement of customer service, reduction of overtime, creation of new policies (floating, for example), improvement in employee satisfaction, reduction of infection rate, etc. In some leadership development programs, this type of learning makes up the bulk of the program (Squazzo, 2009).

For example, the number of falls on your unit has increased. This is an excellent action-learning project to give to one or more of your high-potential staff nurses. You will need to provide him or her with some parameters of the project, such as what type of resources he or she will have access to and the project's time frames. Have him or her think about how he or she might approach the project and come back to you with his or her plan. Provide support to him or her and ask questions about the thought process. He or she will be responsible for building the team, scheduling meetings, doing research, generating a solution, implementing the solution, evaluating its effectiveness, and then presenting the results to management by the due date. The last step in the process will be getting feedback from the team as to his or her leadership and project management skills.

What competencies will the nurse be building through this process? There are many, such as communication, decision-making, analysis, team building, project management, influencing others, and creative and critical thinking. At the end of the project, ask him or her what he or she learned. Give feedback on your observations and offer congratulations for a job well done (assuming it was). Most sound leadership develop-ment programs include some type of action-learning project to culminate the experi-ence and embed new skills.

Coaching

Coaching has been discussed in many of this book's chapters. Observing your staff members and coaching them is one of the best tools for developing future leaders.

> *"A good coach will make his players see what they can become rather than what they are."*
> —*Ara Parseghian*

Mentoring

Most great leaders had mentors who were instrumental in their development. People need guidance, especially when they enter a new organization or role. A mentor is someone who guides another person. Other descriptors include role model, teacher, challenger, cheerleader, coach, and friend (White, Buhr & Pinheiro, 2009). "Mentoring is described as purposeful activities that facilitate the career development, personal growth, caring, empowerment, and nurturance that is integral to nursing practice and leadership" (Wroten & Waite, 2009). Mentoring is broader than coaching, but a mentor and coach can be the same person.

In addition to the goals that were listed previously for leadership development pro-grams—build self-awareness, build organizational and industry understanding, build new skills through learning and application, build leadership confidence—the mentor can also provide the mentee with career support and psychological support (Noe, 2005). According to Noe, career support can come in the form of challenging assign-ments and opportunities for increased exposure and visibility. In addition, the mentor can help with professional value and vision clarification. Psychological support is so important to newcomers. They need someone whom they can trust and talk to and to whom they can ask any question and express their fears and anxieties without fear of retribution. Mentors share their own experiences, successes and failures, and the lessons learned from them. They ask lots of questions to the mentee to get him or her to explore more depth behind his or her decisions and actions, and to consider the effects of decisions and actions on others and him- or herself. In essence, the mentor both focuses the lens down for a micro view and puts on the wide angle lens to be sure the big picture and consequences are considered.

A formal mentoring program is one where mentors and mentees are matched based on mentee needs and mentor expertise. A formal mentoring program ensures that:

- Everyone gets a mentor

- There are specific goals and expectations of the program

- The mentors are agreeable to the goals and expectations and are willing to take the time to mentor

- The mentors are briefed on the benefits of mentoring

- The mentors are trained in how to mentor and in how to begin, terminate, and evaluate the relationship.

In contrast, an informal mentoring program is one where the dyad forms a mentoring relationship on their own. Since it is still typical that most organizations do not have a formal mentoring program, most mentoring relationships are informal and tend to happen by chance. Although most of these relationships are very helpful, you can foresee some potential pitfalls if they are not bounded by the parameters of a formal program.

There are benefits to the mentor as well as the mentee. The process is rewarding. For those who have been guided and helped, it is like "paying it forward." Being of service to others and watching them flourish is deeply gratifying. Mentors pass along their knowledge to those who are less experienced, but questions arise that necessitate that the mentor stretch his or her skills as well. Therefore, mentors always learn during this process. In many cases, deep personal relationships ensue that can last many years.

Nursing is all about caring for others. "Nurses must apply this same principal of human caring to each other. Nurses are first and foremost human, requiring the human relationship of caring support, and encouragement that can come from good mentorship" (Wroten & Waite, 2009).

> *"Better than a thousand days of diligent study is one day with a great teacher."*
> *—Japanese proverb*

References

1. Berglas, S. (2006). "How to keep players productive." *Harvard Business Review*, 84(9), 104–112.

2. Conger, J. A., & Fulmer, R. M. (2003). "Developing your leadership pipeline." *Harvard Business Review*, 81(12), 76–84.

3. Eiser, B. J. A. (2008). "Meeting the challenge of moving from technical expert to leader." *Leadership in Action,* 28(5), 13–24.

4. Hudson, T. (2008). "Delegation: Building a foundation for our future nurse leaders." *Medsurg Nursing,* 17(6), 396–412.

5. McAlearney, A. S., Fisher, D., Heiser, K., Robbins, D., & Kelliher, K. (2005). "Developing effective physician leaders: Changing cultures and transforming organizations." *Hospital Topics,* 83(2), 11–18.

6. Noe, R. A. (2005). *Employee Training and Development* (3rd ed.). New York: McGraw-Hill/Irwin.

7. Squazzo. J. D. (2009). "Cultivating tomorrow's leaders: Comprehensive development strategies ensure continued success." *Healthcare Executive,* 24(6), 8–20.

8. Wells, W. & Hejna, W. (2009). "Developing leadership talent in healthcare organizations." *Healthcare Financial Management,* 63(1), 66–69.

9. White, H. K., Buhr, G. T., & Pinheiro, S. O. (2009). "Mentoring: A key strategy to prepare the next generation of physicians to care for an aging America." *Journal of the American Geriatrics Society,* 57(7), 1270–1277.

10. Wroten, S. J., & Waite, R. (2009). "A call to action: Mentoring within the nursing profession—a wonderful gift to give and share." *The ABNF Journal,* 20(4), 106–108.

DEVELOPING YOURSELF

Learning Objectives

After reading this chapter, the reader will be able to:

- Describe the benefits of using a 360-degree review to get feedback

- List reasons to engage a coach and a mentor

Just as you focus on developing the talent of your staff, so too do you need to develop yourself even if you have no ambitions for promotion. Everyone has strengths and weaknesses and you need to assess yourself so you can build on your strengths, mitigate your weaker areas, and become a more effective manager and leader.

If your organization doesn't have a talent management system--and most don't (Squazzo, 2009)—don't worry. There are many activities that you can do to develop yourself without being part of a formal organization-sanctioned program. These activities are similar to what was discussed in Chapter 14. Keep in mind that you don't need to begin all the activities simultaneously. Start with building self-awareness and then choose which next development activity makes the most sense for you. Talk to your manager, coach, or mentor to determine which activity will be the most impactful to your success first. Create a two-year plan with his or her input.

Leadership Self-Development Actions

Just as with your staff, you need to build self-awareness through identification of your strengths and weaknesses and a personality assessment; improve your organizational and industry understanding; acquire new skills through learning and application; and boost your leadership confidence.

Build your self-awareness

Great leaders are self-aware. They have a clear understanding of what they are good at and what they are not good at. Start with reflecting on what you feel you do really well and what you do not do well. Take the list of competencies for your position and select the three competencies you feel are key strengths and the three competencies you feel are weaknesses for you. If you don't have a competency model for your position, consider some of the following (about 10 is average):

- Leading others and self

    - Managing change: constantly looks for ways to improve processes and structures to meet goals more effectively and efficiently; understands and implements a thoughtful change process

    - Delegating: looks for projects and tasks that utilize strengths of others or helps to develop skills in others to achieve unit goals and staff development goals

    - Building strong, cohesive teams: keeps team members focused on the goals and promotes interdependence among teammates

    - Inspiring and living the vision: clearly articulates the vision to others; role-models behaviors consistent with the vision

    - Commitment to personal and professional growth: has accurate self-awareness; seeks ways to learn and develop skills; takes risks to practice new behaviors that may be out of the comfort zone

- Interpersonal skills
  - Communication: written and spoken communication is clear, effective, and respectful
  - Managing conflict: recognizes and addresses conflict to preserve and build relationships; demonstrates expertise in expressing and eliciting opposing ideas
  - Executive presence: commands attention and respect; shows respect for others; maintains a confident and calm demeanor even in stressful situations
  - Building relationships across functional areas: builds and maintains trusting relationships with key people across functional areas to build opportunities for collaboration
  - Influencing others: persuades others to adopt an idea or process to enhance organizational or unit objectives

- Management
  - Decision-making: uses a sound decision-making process that involves others; gathers and analyzes information, brainstorms options, selects the best option, implements the solution, and evaluates the results
  - Developing talent: assesses the skill level of current human resources and plans development (including coaching) depending on the individual and group needs and gaps
  - Financial acumen: understands the financial situation of the organization and the implications of activities within the department; operates within budget constraints; makes optimal use of resources
  - Execution: executes the plan
  - Strategic planning: sees the big picture; looks to the future and can identify implications of trends; communicates strategy to the team

After you have identified the areas you feel are your strengths and weaknesses, get some input from others. Have a discussion with your manager to ask what he or she sees as your strengths and weaknesses. Get specific feedback on each. Also talk to your staff and peers. You will likely get slightly different lists from each group since each has opportunities to see different behaviors from you. For example, your peers may not know how much coaching you do with your staff since they may not have the opportunity to observe this behavior. They may not identify this competency as a strength for you.; however, your staff may identify this as strength. Nevertheless, their input, based on their vantage point, will provide valuable input and confirmation or disconfirmation of your self-awareness.

You can gather data through a 360-degree review, and your organizational development (OD) human resources (HR) representative should be able to help you execute this process. If he or she cannot, you can hire an external coach to launch this process for you, debrief the results, and create a development plan.

Another tool to build your self-awareness is a personality or behavioral assessment. Frequently used instruments in leadership development include Hogan, The Birkman Method®, and DISC. There are also several EQ instruments available to measure your "emotional quotient" or "emotional intelligence." Daniel Goleman (1995) defines emotional intelligence as comprising the following: knowing one's emotions, managing emotions, motivating oneself, recognizing emotions in others, and handling relationships. Again, talk to your OD person or your coach to determine which one is best for you.

Improve your organizational and industry understanding

The higher you go in an organization, the more strategic you must be. Even if you have no aspirations for higher levels of leadership, knowing what is going on inside and outside of your organization will enable you to help your staff understand the cascade of changes they are experiencing. The more clearly they see the big picture—both the current and the looming situations—the less stressful the next change will be.

Make it a goal to stay abreast of what is happening inside your organization's walls. Attend leadership meetings, think about what you hear, and ask questions if something doesn't make sense. Build relationships with others in your organization, both within the nursing organization and outside of it.

Stay abreast of what is happening in your community by reading local publications. Pay attention to demographic and industry shifts.

Make sure to also keep up with healthcare reform and its implications to your organization. Stay current with changes in your profession. Attend conferences and apply what makes sense to you.

Acquire new skills through learning and application

Attend training classes that are offered by your hospital. Determine which ones are likely to be most helpful to you and discuss what you learned with your manager, coach, and mentor. Decide how you will apply what you learned within two weeks of the class. If you don't apply what you learned, the binder will go on the shelf and you will forget the key points. With repeated practice, eventually a new skill will become a habit. Make sure to evaluate the effectiveness of your new behavior.

Volunteer to be part of a project team to solve a real problem. If you can't find an opportunity for an action-learning project, ask your manager for advice or create a project yourself and invite others to assist you. This will help you build communication and project management skills and also relationships with others.

Boost your leadership confidence

There are many ways to build leadership confidence, but the two most effective are through coaching and mentoring.

Find yourself a coach, who might be your manager or an executive coach hired from outside the organization. The benefits of having your manager as your coach include his or her ability to observe you in real time. Your manager attends meetings with you and can give you feedback and coaching on your behavior. Receiving specifics on how you communicate and interact with others and manage projects is valuable. Your manager will also be able to assess how you interact with your staff, assuming he or she comes to your unit and your staff meetings on occasion. Also, there will be no additional expenses if your manager coaches you.

You can also consider hiring an executive coach. Executive coaches bring entirely different perspectives and qualifications designed specifically for coaching. Coaching is their full-time job. They will help you reflect on your experiences, behaviors, feelings, and results by asking you well thought out questions. They will help you reframe situations and try new behaviors to get better results. They will hold you accountable to do your assigned homework and help you reach your potential.

Since executive coaching is so valuable in building leadership bench strength, many employers will pay for executive coaches. However, if it isn't in the budget, often people will hire coaches themselves. How do you find an external coach that is right for you? Ask others in your organization whom they have used. Ask your HR department for recommendations. Have an initial meeting with the coach to ask some questions and determine whether their qualifications and style are what you need. Look for a coach who has experience coaching managers and executives in your profession. Find someone who knows healthcare and who has business and leadership acumen. It is very helpful if your coach speaks your language.

Be sure to ask about his or her coaching process, which should include some type of assessment (behavioral, 360-degree tool, etc.) followed by the creation of a development plan. Ask for examples of how the coach has done this in the past and successes he or she has seen.

In addition to a coach, find yourself a mentor if one isn't assigned to you. Typically, mentors work at the same organization as the mentee, but not always. They are successful in their roles and have a desire to pay it forward. They will usually be people who have been at the organization longer than the mentee, are at a higher level, are admired and respected, and have an interest in and the time to help guide you. They may be persons who hold the type of position you aspire to (Schira, 2007).

Your mentor and you should:

- Have goals (networking, understanding the culture, developing leadership confidence, gaining career guidance, etc.)

- Have a regularly scheduled meeting time (once a month, for example); begin and end meetings on time

- Establish the duration of the relationship (start with six months and renew if both are agreeable)

- Exchange résumés

- Keep commitments to each other and keep confidences

- Express appreciation

Mentoring is designed to help increase your skills and confidence, focus your career, and build job satisfaction (Bally, 2007). Mentors will provide the safety net you need to take risks and grow.

> *"It is only out on the limb where the fruit grows."*
> *—Unknown author*

Take risks. It is more comfortable to stay where it is safe, but new ideas, skills, and passions are never generated from the easy chair. Continue your professional and personal development throughout your life so that you can contribute everything you are capable of and reach your potential.

"You will either step forward into growth or you will step back into safety."
—*Abraham Maslow*

You choose. Choose well!

References

1. Bally, J. M. G. (2007). "The role of nursing leadership in creating a mentoring culture in acute care environments." *Nursing Economics*, 25(3), 143–149.

2. Goleman, D. (1995). *Emotional Intelligence: Why It Can Matter More Than IQ*. New York: Bantam Books.

3. Schira, M. (2007). "Leadership: A peak and perk of professional development." *Nephrology Nursing Journal*, 34(3), 289–294.

4. Squazzo, J. D. (2009). "Cultivating tomorrow's leaders." *Healthcare Executive*, 24(6), 8–20

NURSING EDUCATION INSTRUCTIONAL GUIDE

Target Audience

Nurse managers, nurse leaders, directors of nursing, VPs of nursing, chief nursing officers/chief nurse executives, charge nurses, clinical nurse leaders, staff development specialists, directors of staff development, retention coordinators, VPs of patient care services.

Statement of Need

This management resource provides nurse leaders with communication strategies and proven methods to help elevate the performance of their nursing staff. It is written to inspire both new and seasoned nurse leaders to become role models within their organizations and provides specific ways to coach and mentor staff, including dealing with negative performance and keeping top-performing staff committed and engaged. (This activity is intended for individual use only.)

Educational Objectives

Upon completion of this activity, participants should be able to:

- Define authentic leadership
- List the five dimensions of authentic leadership
- Explain why self-awareness is a necessary competency for authentic leaders

- Define organizational culture

- List the three general types of organizational cultures

- Describe how the culture is communicated by and embedded in the organization

- Explain why trust is essential for authentic leaders

- Describe ways to build trusting relationships

- State the steps of a sound interview process

- Describe the benefits of hiring the best

- Describe the difference between goals and expectations

- List some examples of expectations that should be explicit to your staff

- Describe why nonverbal communication is so important

- Explain the steps of the listening process

- Define feedback

- List ways to gather feedback

- Define what is coaching for desirable performance

- List the steps in the coaching process

- Explain the steps to take in a constructive coaching scenario

- Identify the elements of a development plan

- Explain how a confrontation discussion differs from a constructive coaching discussion

- Explain the circumstances under which a confrontation discussion should occur

- State the reasons for conducting thorough performance appraisals

- Identify the benefits for incorporating self-appraisals into the process

- Explain why nurses need to be adaptable

- List barriers to change

- Explain the importance of celebrating success

- Describe how to make celebrations meaningful

- Describe the goals of a good leadership development program

- Explain the benefits of mentoring

- Describe the benefits of using a 360-degree review to get feedback

- List reasons to engage a coach and a mentor

Faculty

Patty Kubus, RN, MBA, PhD, is the President of Leadership Potential International, Inc., which specializes in executive coaching, leadership development, career planning, team building, and cultural change initiatives. Along with her nursing credentials, she has an MBA and a doctorate in human development and education. She was formerly a nurse manager at the University of Rochester Medical Center in New York.

Continuing Education

Nursing Contact Hours:
HCPro, Inc., is accredited as a provider of continuing nursing education by the American Nurses Credentialing Center Commission on Accreditation.

This educational activity for 4 nursing contact hours is provided by HCPro, Inc.

Faculty Disclosure Statement

HCPro, Inc., has confirmed that none of the faculty, contributors, or planners have any relevant financial relationships to disclose related to the content of this educational activity.

Disclosure of Unlabeled Use

This educational activity may contain discussion of published and/or investigational uses of agents that are not indicated by the FDA. HCPro, Inc., does not recommend the use of any agent outside of the labeled indications. The opinions expressed in the educational activity are those of the faculty and do not necessarily represent the views of HCPro, Inc. Please refer to the official prescribing information for each product for discussion of approved indications, contraindications, and warnings.

Instructions

In order to be eligible to receive your nursing contact hours for this activity, you are required to do the following:

1. Read the book *Lead! Becoming an Effective Coach and Mentor to Your Nursing Staff*

2. Complete the exam and receive a passing score of 80% or higher

3. Complete the evaluation

4. Provide your contact information on the exam and evaluation

5. Submit the exam and evaluation to HCPro, Inc.

Please provide all of the information requested above and mail or fax your completed exam, program evaluation, and contact information to:

HCPro, Inc.
Attention: Continuing Education Manager
75 Sylvan Street, Suite A-101
Danvers, MA 01923
Fax: 781/639-2982

Note: This book and associated exam are intended for individual use only. If you would like to provide this continuing education exam to other members of your nursing or physician staff, please contact our customer service department at 877/727-1728 to place your order. The exam fee schedule is as follows:

Exam Quantity	Fee
1	$0
2 – 25	$15 per person
26 – 50	$12 per person
51 – 100	$8 per person
101+	$5 per person

Continuing Education Exam

Name: _____

Title: _____

Facility name: _____

Address: _____

Address: _____

City: _____ State: _____ ZIP: _____

Phone number: _____ Fax number: _____

E-mail: _____

Date completed: _____

1. Decision-making, building trust, and prioritizing tasks are made easier by:
   a. Knowing your motivation
   b. Knowing your values
   c. Understanding your need for power
   d. Clearly defining your strengths and weaknesses

2. Important behaviors of authentic leadership include all of the following *except:*
   a. Being self-aware
   b. Being self-disciplined
   c. Being "in flow"
   d. Knowing your leadership purpose

3. Which of the following is a definition of organizational culture?
   a. Culture is "the way we do things around here"
   b. Culture is a representation of the artifacts of the organization
   c. Culture is defined by the external environment
   d. Culture is a pattern of reactions to change

4. Which of the following is *not* a general descriptor of a type of organizational culture?
   a. Aggressive-defensive
   b. Passive-defensive
   c. Constructive
   d. Perfectionistic

5. Which of the following is the most effective way to embed values into a culture?

    a. Artifacts

    b. Role modeling by leaders

    c. Structures and processes

    d. Socialization process

6. Trust is essential for authentic leaders for all of the following reasons *except*:

    a. Influencing others

    b. Effecting change

    c. Empowering others

    d. Maintaining the status quo

7. Open communication, keeping commitments and confidences, achieving competencies, and recognizing accomplishments and contributions are all ways to:

    a. Repair trust

    b. Build trust

    c. Empower others

    d. Role model the culture

8. Which of the following is not one of the steps in the interviewing process?

    a. Know who you are looking for

    b. Use a structured interview process

    c. Explain your expectations

    d. Get some coaching on your interviewing skills

9. Why is it so important to hire the best?

    a. The best hire will be productive more quickly, enjoy more job satisfaction, and will tend to stay with you during good times and bad

    b. If you like their style, they will be easier to manage

    c. So that they fit well with your team

    d. So that they can be promoted sooner

10. If it is specific, measurable, achievable, relevant, and time-bound, it is an:
    a. Objective
    b. Expectation
    c. Goal
    d. Metric

11. Expectations should be explicitly communicated to your staff, both verbally and in writing, around all of the following topics *except:*
    a. How we treat each other
    b. How we resolve disagreements
    c. How we schedule our time
    d. How we determine training budgets

12. Which of the following statements about nonverbal communication is *not* true?
    a. Nonverbal communication consists of visual and vocal elements
    b. Nonverbal communication makes up 7% of the meaning of the message
    c. Vocal elements can include volume, pace, tone, and inflections
    d. People will always believe your nonverbal communication before they believe the content of your communication

13. Listening to others involves which of the following activities?
    a. Holding your agenda in the forefront of your mind
    b. Remaining passive and hearing what is being said
    c. Clearing your mind and listening for both feelings and content
    d. Using the time to prepare your next comment

14. Feedback is:
    a. Describing what someone is doing and what he or she could do differently
    b. Describing the situation, what someone is doing, and the effect of his or her action
    c. Saying "good job"
    d. Letting someone know that his or her actions are not effective

15. All of the following are ways to gather feedback *except:*

    a. Asking patients whether their nurse is meeting their needs

    b. Asking a nurse's colleagues for his or her strengths and development areas

    c. Reviewing care plans

    d. Providing a list of competencies to physicians

16. Coaching for desirable performance is:

    a. Feedback plus reinforcement of positive behaviors

    b. The same as feedback

    c. Feedback plus letting the person know what they have done wrong

    d. Giving the person a pat on the back

17. The coaching process includes all of the following steps *except:*

    a. Sharing feedback

    b. Asking for input

    c. Describing what coachees could do differently

    d. Gathering data

18. Which of the following is *not* an element of a thorough development plan?

    a. Identification of the skill or competency under focus

    b. Identification of activities to be completed and dates of completion for each activity

    c. Identification of benefits to the coachee, unit, and organization

    d. Annual competency assessment

19. Which of the following does *not* pertain to the step "*Coach for desired behavior and desired effect*"?

    a. Empathize when appropriate

    b. Create a development plan

    c. Describe what a desired behavior would have been in that situation

    d. Describe what the effect of the desired behavior would have likely been

20. An employee or colleague needs to be confronted:
    a. After making a mistake
    b. If they have violated a policy or a standard or expectation that makes their behavior unsafe or disruptive
    c. If they are late completing their charting
    d. If they are unsure how to manage a project

21. How does a confrontation discussion differ from a constructive coaching discussion?
    a. The behavior in question must change immediately
    b. The behavior is not contributing to the person's professional development
    c. The confrontation discussion happens during annual performance reviews
    d. The confrontation discussion is an annual competency

22. Which is a benefit of conducting thorough performance appraisals?
    a. It gives employees an opportunity to gain feedback and clarity on their performance
    b. It gives managers a venue to bring up examples of poor performance that occurred during the last year
    c. It gives employees an opportunity to discuss their feeling about their peers
    d. It gives managers an opportunity to lay out employees' career paths

23. An employee should fill out a self-appraisal prior to the performance appraisal discussion for all the following reasons *except:*
    a. It provides an opportunity for them to reflect on their performance
    b. It helps them be ready to sway the manager toward better ratings
    c. It allows them to become part of the discussion, which is intended to be a two-way street
    d. It helps them think about goals achieved in the past year and what they want to achieve in the coming year, which may include items of which the manager is unaware

24. Nurses need to be adaptable to change for all of the following reasons *except:*
    a. Technology is changing at breakneck pace
    b. Demographics and patients' demands are changing
    c. Patient confidentiality will cease to be an issue with electronic medical records (EMR)
    d. Standards of practice are changing

25. Which of the following is a barrier to change?
    a. Misaligned structures and processes
    b. Tenure of staff
    c. Thoughtfully planned communications
    d. Multifunctional integration

26. Celebrations are an important ingredient in authentic leadership because:
    a. Celebrations help people feel significant and connected to the group
    b. Celebrations allow people to get their minds off work for a while
    c. Celebrations are meant to honor only those who have met goals
    d. Celebrations make leaders look like they care

27. To be sure that your celebrations are meaningful to your staff:
    a. Research what other organizations do to celebrate and then do that
    b. Gather a task force of your staff to create a celebration process for your unit
    c. Think about celebration rituals that you have found to be significant and implement those activities
    d. Come up with a plan, then survey your staff to determine what they like and dislike

28. A good leadership development program will allow the organization to realize the following goals:
    a. Retain strong performers
    b. Build strong clinical skills
    c. Improve relations between nurses and physicians
    d. Improve patient satisfaction

© 2010 HCPro, Inc.

29. The goals of mentoring others include all of the following *except:*
    a. To build confidence
    b. To build a network
    c. To clarify values and build skills
    d. To solve personal issues

30. What benefits can you gain from participating in a 360-degree tool survey?
    a. You have an overview that ties into your compensation package
    b. You gain a clear understanding of how your staff see your strengths and weaknesses
    c. You are able to evaluate the strengths and weaknesses of everyone on your team
    d. You have an overview of the senior leadership in your organization

31. In what ways can you benefit from engaging a coach and a mentor?
    a. You receive a positive performance review
    b. You have help with writing staff performance reviews
    c. You can share your workload with another person
    d. You receive trusted advice to help you take risks that support your growth

Continuing Education Exam Answer Key

(Please record all exam and evaluation answers here)

Name:	License #:
Facility:	Title:
Address:	

City:	State:	ZIP:

Phone:	E-mail: (Certificates are e-mailed to learners unless otherwise stated here)

Please record the letter of the correct answer to the corresponding exam question below:

1.	7.	13.	19.	25.	31.
2.	8.	14.	20.	26.	
3.	9.	15.	21.	27.	
4.	10.	16.	22.	28.	
5.	11.	17.	23.	29.	
6.	12.	18.	24.	30.	

Continuing Education Evaluation

1 = Strongly Agree	2 = Agree	3 = Disagree	4 = Strongly Disagree

Please rate the responses below according to the scale above to rate the quality of this educational activity.

1. Please indicate how well you feel this activity met the learning objectives listed:
   ❏ 1   ❏ 2   ❏ 3   ❏ 4

2. Objectives were related to the overall purpose/goal of the activity:
   ❏ 1   ❏ 2   ❏ 3   ❏ 4

3. This activity was related to my continuing education needs:

❏ 1   ❏ 2   ❏ 3   ❏ 4

4. The exam for the activity was an accurate test of the knowledge gained:

❏ 1   ❏ 2   ❏ 3   ❏ 4

5. The activity avoided commercial bias or influence:

❏ 1   ❏ 2   ❏ 3   ❏ 4

6. This activity met my expectations:

❏ 1   ❏ 2   ❏ 3   ❏ 4

7. The format was an appropriate method for delivery of the content for this activity:

❏ 1   ❏ 2   ❏ 3   ❏ 4

8. Will this activity enhance your professional practice?

❏ Yes   ❏ No

9. How much time did it take for you to complete this activity?

_____

10. Do you have any additional comments on this activity?

_____

_____

_____

Return completed form to:

HCPro, Inc. • Attention: Continuing Education Manager • 75 Sylvan Street, Suite A-101 • Danvers, MA 01923
Telephone: 877/727-1728 • Fax: 781/639-2982